Brierley's Liverpool

'The Changing Face of a City'

David Brazendale
Additional material by John Tiernan

Copy 020 of 100

To Jutta and Morten
with special Thanks
David Brazendale
March 2018

Published by The Athenaeum, Liverpool

ISBN number   978-1-5272-1820-8

This book is dedicated to all past and present Proprietors of The Athenaeum 1797–2017

Patrons of Brierley's Liverpool

Contents

Foreword by the late Sir Alan Waterworth (1931 – 2016)

Since they were purchased in 1830, James Brierley's characteristic drawings of Liverpool buildings and streets have been housed in the Athenaeum, available to researchers, but not on public view. Their publication now is an exciting event for the ever-growing number of people interested in our city's history.

These drawings are the first to give us a clear idea of what the streets, warehouses and shops of early nineteenth-century Liverpool really looked like. Enfield's History of Liverpool, published in Warrington in 1773, has only one such scene – the fine, atmospheric view of The Custom House from Trafford's Wynt – but neither the wood engravings in Troughton's Liverpool (1810), nor the lithographs of S. & G. Nicholson (1821), conveys any idea of how the town itself looked.

W. G. Herdman's Ancient Liverpool (1843) was consciously concerned with recapturing scenes and buildings which had already passed away. Locally, the only artist accurately delineating contemporary street views was G. Batenham of Chester who published his collection of twenty four etchings of that city in 1817, eight years before Brierley produced the first of his drawings.

It is both fortunate and appropriate that David Brazendale, who has written extensively on local history and is himself not only a Proprietor of the Athenaeum but also Chairman of the Library Sub-Committee, should have agreed to contribute the valuable text that so enhances these historic drawings.

The book is a significant contribution to our knowledge of Liverpool, especially the area around the Old Dock which, at the time Brierley was making his drawings, was soon to be redeveloped.

Alan Waterworth, KCVO, MA, LLD, JP,
Former Lord Lieutenant of Merseyside

BETTELEY

KING STREET

ANDREWS & Cº

Pool Lane, now South Castle Street.

Introduction & Acknowledgement

Since its inception in 1797, the Athenaeum in Liverpool has been a centre of learning and a repository for all matters and material related to the growth and history of the town. One of the largest sections of the library is a collection of books relating to Liverpool, together with an extensive assemblage of pamphlets, papers, pictures and documents. The original impetus for the acquisition of local material may have come from John Jones, who had been appointed as Librarian on Thursday 3 October 1822. It might be thought that the membership of the Athenaeum would have been unwilling to take the recommendations of an employee, but Jones was a man who seems to have been very highly regarded by the Proprietors. In July 1829, when he was suffering from ill-health, the Committee graciously granted him 14 days' leave of absence, with an optional week's extension, a tolerance that is in noted contrast to their attitude to Mr Lloyd, Master of the News Room, whose duties commenced at 7 a.m., and continued until the institution closed at 10 p.m. It was only with reluctance that it was agreed that Lloyd should have two hours' leave a day. Mr Jones was also permitted to live in his own house and was given latitude in the purchasing policy and organisation of the library. Further testimony to the regard in which John Jones was held came in 1831. In November of that year, the General Committee,

Assembled for the first time after the death of the late Librarian Mr Jones, without recording their deep regret for the loss which the Institution has suffered by that event and that it only remains for them to hope that his successor will study to emulate the extraordinary zeal, assiduity and integrity which distinguished that excellent individual.
(Athenaeum Minute Book, vol. 1.)

A man so well respected and valued for his scholarship may have easily persuaded the Proprietors that the establishment of a collection of local topographical views was a worthy aim. In June 1827 we find a record of 'The purchase of etchings of various Liverpool scenes taken from the 'British Traveller' at cost of £3 16s. 9d.' [£3.84.] On 22 June 1830 the sum of £2 12s. 6d. [£2.62] was spent on twenty-one views of churches by Brierley at 2s. 6d. [12p] per picture. The subjects of these pictures are listed and can be identified as those in the present collection, with the exception of depictions of the churches of St Peter and St Nicholas, which have been lost. The only non-ecclesiastical picture in this group was that of the Van Dries Coffee House. On 9 September 1830, another 49 pictures by Brierley, purchased by Jones, were delivered. These are listed and can be identified as the heart of the present collection. They were purchased at prices varying from 2s. 6d. [12p] to 1s. [5p] at a total cost of £4 15s. 0d. [£4.75]. On 1 December of the same year, 24 further views were obtained at a charge of £3 0s. 0d.

It is not apparent from the records if, when commissioning the pictures, Jones was acting on his own initiative or carrying out instructions from his employers. Equally, the selection of subjects remains a matter of speculation. However, we can surmise that the Librarian and the Proprietors were anxious to make a topographical record of a town that was changing daily, as Liverpool shed its past and was being rebuilt as a modern, commercial city. That this was the intention is supported by the fact that Brierley mainly depicts buildings and streets which were liable to almost immediate demolition and redevelopment. It is remarkable that of the several hundred buildings depicted by Brierley only one, St Luke's Church, survives today, and that only in a ruined state. Thus we have a unique record of Liverpool in a period of which few, if any, traces remain.

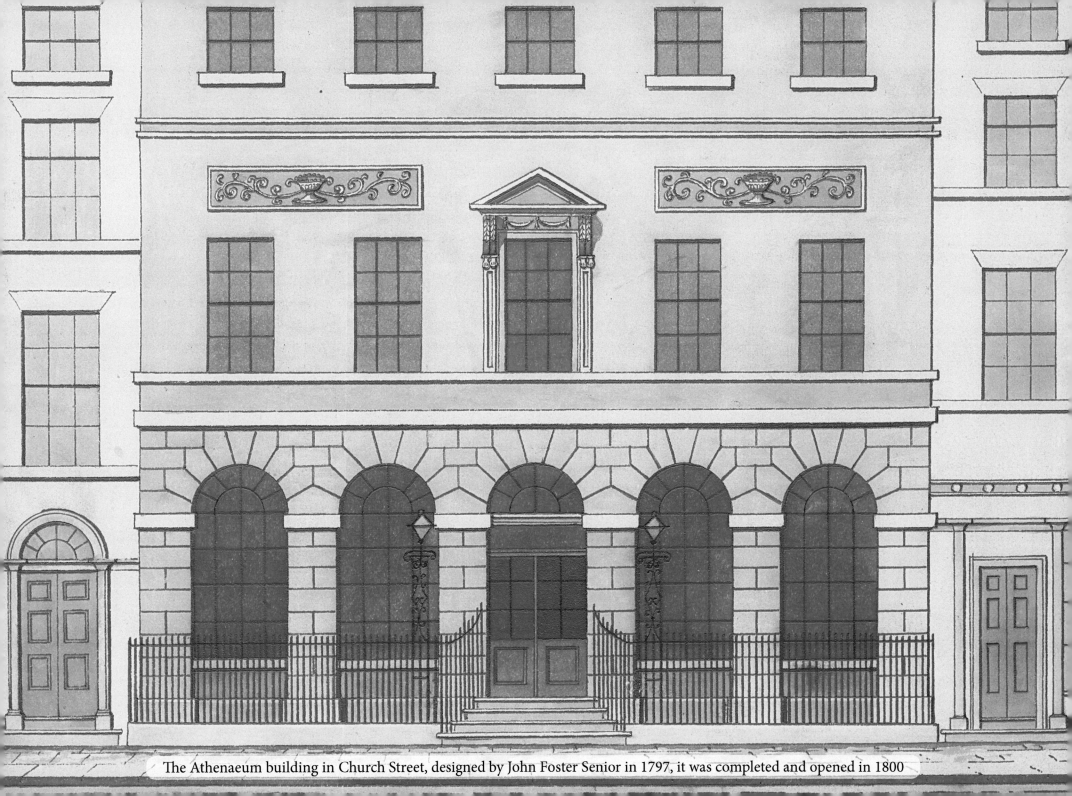

The Athenaeum building in Church Street, designed by John Foster Senior in 1797, it was completed and opened in 1800

John Jones, Librarian of the Athenaeum d.1831
Librarian from October 1822, Jones served in the post until his death in 1831. During his period in office, Jones seems to have directed the policy of the Institution towards the establishment of a collection of local material.

In the period 1820–30 Liverpool was in a transitional phase. The great expansion during the Georgian era that had transformed a small coastal town into an entrepôt with world-wide trading links, revelling in a new-found prosperity, was passed. The great boom period of the later nineteenth century had yet to begin and Brierley's pen and brush record the last days of the old town before its remnants were swept away in the great Victorian re-building. It was this period which saw the conversion of the old town centre from a mixture of residential and business property into a resplendent commercial and mercantile development. The Brierley decade is poised on the cusp of the introduction of steam-powered transport by rail and sea which was to revolutionise trade and the movement of peoples throughout the world. The fact that the collection was made may be taken to suggest that the membership of the Athenaeum felt a nostalgia for the old town in which they had grown up. On the other hand, it was men of the class from which the Proprietors were drawn who were instrumental in the development of the new town and who were to be the occupiers of the new buildings that were springing up. Perhaps their pleasure in 'progress' was tempered by a regard for the past. Evidently, Brierley, about whom so little is known, had some reputation in Liverpool for topographical drawings of this type, a reputation sufficient to cause him to be commissioned by Thomas Binns to supply 163 drawings, many of which are of similar subjects to those shown in the Athenaeum's collection. Binns lived on Mount Vernon and, with his partner Isaac Hadwen, had a business as a leather merchant in Pool Lane. He was an avid antiquarian and collector whose collection of Brierley drawings is now held in the Liverpool Central Library.

The Brierley pictures in the Athenaeum, when considered alongside the directories of the period, can give us a uniquely detailed picture of areas of Liverpool at this time in its history. In addition to the information that they give about the streets of Liverpool in 1830 they also open a door to clues about the development and growth of the town and in various ways, help us to recall many fast disappearing aspects of local life. Where possible it has been thought necessary to develop these insights so that this is not just a book about the Brierley drawings but a record of the diverse aspects of Liverpool's history during a seminal period of its development.

In preparing this book extensive use has been made of contemporary printed sources, of which the most useful have been the street directories of the period. The first published directory for Liverpool was issued by the stationer, John Gore, in 1766, though a manuscript directory for 1734 is held in the Athenaeum collection. The decision to publish a directory reflected both the increasing size of the town and its enhanced commercial importance. After 1766 the directory was an annual publication, under various proprietors, until the late twentieth century.

Gore's Directories are much more than a simple listing of residents with their addresses and occupations. To this are added sections of useful commercial information concerning transport and services, market regulations, information on tides and details of coastal vessels, and the names and locations of various local officials. There are also descriptions of churches, public buildings and institutions. Finally, Gore included a section of 'Annals' where a year by year calendar of events in Liverpool is listed. Various other sections contain information of a less substantial nature, ranging from cab fares to the revival of drowned persons.

For this book most use has been made of Gore's Directory for 1829, as it coincides most closely with Brierley's work. The directories do not include a reverse directory with lists of the occupants of each individual street. Without such a listing, an attempt to identify the occupier of an individual property would necessitate a search through every name in the directory.

The problem is alleviated by the work of Edward Baines (1774–1848). He was a journalist, antiquarian and publisher of many books on history and topography as well as political and instructional works. His History, Directory and Gazatteer [sic] for the County Palatine of Lancaster was published in 1824/5 and is a work of tremendous industry. All the principal towns of Lancashire are described and several have accompanying plans. A version of the history of the county as a whole and of each town in particular is given, together with a list of residents and a classified directory of trades and professions. Most importantly for our purposes it includes a list of the inhabitants of the principal streets. The latter has proved invaluable and can be shown to coincide with remarkable accuracy with the depiction of the same street by Brierley. Baines presented a copy of the work to the Athenaeum and the vote of thanks to him is recorded in the Minutes of 1825 [Athenaeum Minute Book vol. 1].

When preparing notes on each picture, extensive use has been made of the list of the occupants of a street, where this is available. Each house was identified and the residents listed by comparison with the main directory listing. A problem is the frequency with which premises changed hands. A comparison between the directories for 1825 and 1829 shows wholesale changes, at least in the threatened streets chosen as subjects by James Brierley. After making a list of the inhabitants, the names were compared with the directory section, thus obtaining a note of their occupation and, in many cases, the residence of the proprietor of a business. In a few cases, reference has then been made to the lists of classified occupations which may give additional details. The list of occupiers was then compared with that of Gore's Directory for 1829. It is this correlation which allows for the observations on the frequent changes in businesses and their owners.

The fact that Brierley includes so many shop names, sign boards and fascias – ninety are shown in the various pictures – has been found to provide an essential clue to identifying which portion of a particular street he is depicting. On one or two occasions the names he gives have not been found to be substantiated by any directory.

Another deficiency of the directories as an historical source is that not everybody was included in the lists. The names shown are confined to the 'respectable' section of the population: persons with a business, however small, shop keepers, tradesmen, manufacturers, merchants, gentlemen and ladies. The lower orders, however, are disregarded. From the directory we get no impression of the teeming slums, the over-crowed courts and the abominable cellar dwellings for which Liverpool became notorious and where, two years after Brierley made his drawings, the cholera epidemic caused so many deaths.

No book of this size and complexity can be created without the help and participation of many people to whom I must express my appreciation and gratitude. Principally, my thanks go to my fellow Proprietors and members of the Athenaeum and especially the members of Library Sub-Committee, for the encouragement and help I have received. I must thank my collaborator, Mr John Tiernan for his invaluable contribution of the chapter outlining the history of the Athenaeum and its library. I have been assisted by the presidents of the Athenaeum who have held office during the time the project has been proceeding. I express my thanks to Dr. Ian Cubbin and Mr Jack Birley whose persistence and determination have brought the book to publication. Mr Vincent Roper and Mrs Joan Hanford have selflessly shared their extensive knowledge of the collections. I extend my thanks to Mr Roger Hull and the staff of the Liverpool Record Office. An invaluable contribution was made by Ms Caroline Raynor of Oxford Archaeology. Caroline shared her experience in the excavations of the Old Dock and its surrounding areas and provided several illustrations of the work. It is gratifying that the Athenaeum was able to repay her by providing illustrative material for the visitor's centre at the site While I have wandered the streets of early nineteenth century Liverpool, my wife Hilary, my assiduous proof reader, my sternest critic, and most generous supporter, has kept me in touch with the twenty-first century. My thanks and appreciation goes to her for this and so much else.

While many have contributed to this work, any errors are entirely my responsibility.

James Brierley - The Threshold Decade 1820–1830

The renaissance of Liverpool in the Georgian era was to give way to its huge expansion and development in the Victorian and Edwardian periods as 'Second City of the Empire'. Perhaps it was a perception that this change was imminent which inspired Brierley and the Proprietors of the Athenaeum to try to record the old town. In an age when photography was in its birth pangs, the only medium by which this could be achieved was by the pen and brush of the artist. Brierley's drawings show the last glimpses of the old town of Liverpool, authentic depictions of the individual streets and buildings, recorded with an almost photographic accuracy, showing places as they were.

Many of these drawings are dated 1830 and it was the events of September 15 of that year which saw the beginning of the modern world with its emphasis on the speedy, mass transport of goods and people. On that morning, from the new terminus station at Crown Street on the top of Brownlow Hill, a great procession of locomotives pulling decorated coaches set out through the Moorish Arch on a journey intended to mark the ceremonial and triumphal opening of the Liverpool and Manchester Railway, a project fraught with difficulties and nine years in completion. The departure was marked by the usual panoply of bands, bunting and cheering crowds. The parade was led by the Northumbrian, with George Stephenson himself at the controls, pulling the triumphal car of the Duke of Wellington.

Plans to improve the communications between the two emerging metropolitan centres of the industrial age and to supplement the inadequate water and road links had been discussed for many years. The implementation of the railway plan had been driven on by a body of directors, mainly drawn from the Liverpool corn merchants, notably Joseph Sandars, James Cropper and Henry Booth (Athenaeum Proprietor No. 337), who, in 1823, began to take steps to bring the proposals to realisation. Liverpool was a town where numbers of wealthy men were anxious to seize the opportunities for the improved communication provided by the technological advances of the

period and had embraced the canal age with enthusiasm. On this September day, the 'Railway Age' with its enormous and world-changing effects on society, on employment, on communication, on industrial development and on the reduction in regionalism had begun; and Brierley's Liverpool was at its heart.

Opening of the Liverpool and Manchester Railway

At least two other transport projects for Liverpool were mooted at this period. In May 1827 the Corporation considered a proposal from James Lowe for the construction of 'a tunnel under the Mersey from Liverpool to Cheshire'. Perhaps wisely, it was resolved that any opinion on this subject could not be given without plans and other documents and that, when these were produced, the matter would be given due consideration. It was to be a hundred years before a plan was put into effect, although the railway tunnel to Birkenhead was completed in 1886.

In 1828 yet another proposal to facilitate the Mersey crossing was put forward. On 2 July the Corporation: 'Received a report, accompanied by plans from Messrs Twyford and Wilson of Manchester, relative to a bridge being placed across, the River Mersey opposite Birkenhead having been laid before the Council, (and) Resolved, that the subject is one of too great importance with reference to the navigation of the river for this Council to give any reply to the same without the further opinion of and report of some of the most eminent civil engineers of the day, being obtained by the promoters of the measure.' Either they were advised against such a scheme or the opinion of the eminent engineers was never obtained, as no more was heard of the proposal.

As the world entered this period of change, Liverpool was undergoing a metamorphosis. The previous hundred years had seen the town emerge as a great port and a centre of commerce. It had undergone a cultural development from a place obsessed with shipping and trade, where the main preoccupation of its inhabitants was a drive for monetary success, relieved by bucolic and alcoholic entertainment, into a place where cultural pursuits were supported, at least by 'The Quality'. The myth of the 'Liverpool Gentleman' as opposed to the 'Manchester Man' had been born. The tutelary genius of this cultural revolution was William Roscoe (1753–1831) (Athenaeum Proprietor No. 2). This autodidactic polymath, described by his latest biographer as 'Historian, writer, poet, art patron and collector, botanist, Member of Parliament and anti-slavery campaigner … has been widely acclaimed as the founding father of Liverpool culture' (William Roscoe, Commerce and Culture, A. Wilson, Liverpool 2008). Amongst his other contributions to his home town was the significant part he played in the foundation of the Academy of Arts, the Royal Institution, the Botanic Gardens, and the Athenaeum, where his memory is still honoured.

William Roscoe 1753-1821
William Roscoe was largely self-educated and became the leading scholar and artistic patron in Liverpool. Internationally known as a historian, poet, botanist, and political activist. [Athenaeum Proprietor No. 2]

During the decade 1820–30, this emergent interest in artistic activities is perceptible in the records of the Corporation, which was now prepared to recognise the arts as worthy of civic patronage, particularly if the artist was a local talent. James Brierley was only one of a number of artists practising in the town. In August 1828, the Council decided to offer a premium of twenty guineas each for the best work of painting, drawing and sculpture 'executed by artists resident in Liverpool' displayed at the exhibition organised by the Royal Institution: one wonders if Brierley competed for this prize. By the following year they were more generous and offered a prize of £20 for the best historical picture and landscape, while the best watercolour and the best carving in alto or basso relievo were to receive £12 each. Smaller sums were to be awarded to students and artists resident in Liverpool who were not members of the Liverpool Academy. The city fathers were prepared to encourage and patronise distinguished artists of national reputation. On 4 July 1821, they sought permission from the Duke of York to commission a portrait of his Highness by 'one of the most eminent artists of the day'. However, plans sometimes went awry and it was 'Resolved that the Mayor … be requested to communicate to Sir Thomas Lawrence the great dissatisfaction felt by this Council at not having finished the portrait of his late Majesty, particularly so as from the strong and repeated assurances from Sir Thomas, they have been induced to believe it would be finished.' Though the debates are not recorded in detail the impression is given that the solid burghers who made up the Corporation 'knew what they liked' when it came to art and were not enthusiastic for the fanciful. When John Smith suggested that the Council should purchase 'a beautiful piece of sculpture by the late Mr John Deare, a native of the town', a sculptor worthy of an entry in the Dictionary of National Biography – 'representing the marriage of Thetis and Peleus to be placed in the Town Hall' - they promptly turned down the opportunity.

A feature of the Liverpool cultural scene had for many years been the annual music festivals which featured the great northern tradition of choral music and oratorio. These events were originally staged in churches, before a concert hall was established by 1786. This proved inadequate and in 1827 the Corporation received a memorial 'numerously and respectably signed by inhabitants of the town', asking that plans for a large hall appropriate for the use of the music festivals and other purposes should be considered. This petition eventually initiated the planning and building of the great St George's Hall.

Another lively aspect of the Liverpool cultural and social scene was the theatre. The Theatre Royal (see page 95) in Williamson Square features in one of Brierley's most impressive drawings. Between 1820 and 1830 it had seen performances by some of the most distinguished stage personalities of the age – Charles Macready, Edmund Keene and Charles Kemble had all appeared.

In July 1827 a Miss Glover took the title role in a performance of Hamlet and was described in the review in the Liverpool Theatrical Investigator as 'a very obese prince'! In 1823 the worlds of the theatre and of the music festival clashed, exposing the undercurrent of violence that underlay much of Liverpool's society. The theatre management had given permission for many of their performers to sing in the various day-time concerts that formed part of the festival. However, they had refused permission to a much-admired star, Miss Cranmer. She defied the ban and was dismissed. Her non-appearance at that evening's performance in the theatre sparked a riot and the building suffered severe damage.

For many people in Liverpool their social and cultural lives were to revolve around their church or chapel, which not only sought to fulfil their spiritual needs but also provided a wide range of activities designed to build fellowship and cohesion. The creation of loyalty to church or chapel was especially important at a time when competition between denominations and individual churches was at its height. During the previous century, the Church of England had been a moribund institution, firmly entrenched in the Establishment; being a resort for the middle classes and a source of occupation for the sons of the gentry and aristocracy. Protected by law, the Church of England had sunk into torpor and lethargy and seemed, in general, to be indifferent to the changes in society and population that had been brought about by the industrialisation of England. The industrial worker and the urban poor were often neglected. In contrast, the Non-conformist churches had often become the province of the industrial, commercial and urban elite. However, the dissenting churches were susceptible to division and secessions; the proliferation of chapels often being the result of such factional in-fighting.

The emergence of the Methodist movement after 1784 and the astonishing response elicited from the urban and rural poor by John Wesley, George Whitefield and others, inspired the Church of England to seek methods of evangelism. A new wing emerged in the Church devoted to this mission. One of its earliest and most prominent members was John Newton, preacher and hymn writer, who had a long-standing connection to Liverpool. Between

1833 and 1845 another tendency in the church emerged from the preaching of Keble, Newman, Pusey and others of the Oxford Movement, devoted to returning the Church of England to its pre-reformation Catholic roots and rejecting Protestant Anglicanism. One of the most striking features in Brierley's depictions of Liverpool is the plethora of churches. This profusion reflects differences in practice and approach but also in the social status of church congregations. The diarist and letter writer, Ellen Weeton, was driven from the congregation of St Catherine's in the Temple by her sense of social inadequacy. Liverpool had a large number of wealthy families whose prestige and reputation would be improved by a display of piety. To endow a church was to place a mark on the landscape and increase one's social standing. Another incentive came from the factions within the church which caused patrons to wish for a place of worship that represented their view of the controversies of the day. In addition, the Corporation, growing prosperous on rents and the dock dues, conscious of the increasing extent of the town and the growing number of its inhabitants, was prepared to provide ecclesiastical accommodation for its citizens. Due to the Tory–Anglican inclination of the Corporation it was establishments of the Church of England that they saw fit to build. As a result Liverpool, which had been served until 1734 by only two churches, St Peter's and St Nicholas', had by 1829 nineteen Anglican churches within the town's boundaries. Most of these are subjects of Brierley's pictures. Remarkably, there was a floating chapel for seamen in George's Dock, the chaplain of which was William Scoresby FRS, the distinguished arctic explorer.

There was a wide range of Scottish and Welsh congregations scattered through the town. The Methodists had chapels in Pall Mall and Bedford Street, as well as Leeds Street, Mount Pleasant, Pitt Street, Murray Street and Moses Street; while Baptist chapels were located in Byrom Street, Lime Street, Church Lane and Great Crosshall Street. The main Unitarian Chapel was in Paradise Street but there were other congregations in Renshaw Street and Hunter Street. The Quaker Meeting House was also located in Hunter Street. In addition to Protestant congregations of various hues, there were five Roman Catholic Churches, including St Peter's in Seel Street, built in

1788, now the oldest surviving ecclesiastical building in the city centre. Apart from the Jewish synagogue in Seel Street, no other non-Christian places of worship are included in the Directory. Church allegiance, the world of the arts, theatre and music were only of interest to a small proportion of the ever-growing population of Liverpool. The census returns of 1821 showed there to be 118,000 inhabitants. By the end of the decade this had increased to 123,000 and most of these residents sought their entertainment in a more rumbustious fashion. Writing in 1853 about the period 1775–1800 Richard Brooke says: 'The amusements and habits of the lower classes in Liverpool were then rude and coarse. Drunkenness was a common vice and was indulged in without concealment.' There is no reason to suppose things had changed much by the 1820s. Baines' Directory of 1824 lists no fewer than 1,467 hotels, inns and taverns which were, no doubt, well patronised.

There was a streak of morbid enjoyment in the Liverpool population and shipwrecks, fires and natural disasters were eagerly reported. Events such as the wreck of the Lord Moira packet (1821) on the shores of Wirral during a great storm, the sinking of the landing stage, (which drowned five persons), and the loss of the Dublin packet Alert in 1823 provoked much grisly joy. It seems likely that the crowds who turned out to watch the ascent by the veteran balloonist Charles Green, as an attraction of the Music Festival of 1827, did so in the hope of seeing him crash – they were to be disappointed.

The ever-increasing population of the town was drawn from many places at home and abroad. The town had several settled communities whose origins lay beyond the local district, drawn from Europe and the Mediterranean, from Ireland, Scotland and Wales. However, the majority was from Lancashire, Cheshire and other parts of England. It is calculated that in 1831 at least ten per cent of the population had their origins across the Irish Sea. This is before the great exodus of the Irish Famine years and many of these incomers, according to the Minutes of the Vestry Committee, were skilled workers. However, not all of them belonged to this group and many families who had been itinerant workers and field gangs found their way through Liverpool. These migrants posed a serious problem for the Vestry (See page 25).

At a Special Vestry meeting held in St Nicholas' Church on 10 March 1825, the following minute was made: 'The passing of Irish vagrants to their own country has for some time been extremely burdensome to this Parish; for although the charge ought finally to fall on the County, the fees procuring the necessary documents being considerably more than the expense of direct removal have proved a serious obstacle to repayment.' The theme of the 'Irish Problem' is taken up in the Vestry of 31 October 1826 to explain the increased numbers in the workhouse. The Vestry recorded that

Upwards of 7000 persons have been passed this year from Liverpool to Ireland (of which 3343 were by this parish), many of whom have travelled from the most southern counties, some even from Bristol, which port, as well as London, should relieve this county from a great portion of these vagrants, as numbers of them, either from sickness, absolute want or arriving here in the last stages of pregnancy become a serious burden on the Parish. Others perhaps encouraged by the many humane institutions established in this town, resort hither for the mere purpose of availing themselves of their bounty, especially the Ladies' Charity.

This charity had been founded in 1796 for the 'relief of poor married women in childbed in their own homes'. It was supported by the wives of the great and the good and by 1821 had dealt with a total of 26,845 cases, a yearly average of 1075. Additionally, the charity had provided for the vaccination of 1066 children. It is easy to feel cynical about the work of this sort of organisation, seeing their members as the upper class ladies playing the Lady Bountiful, but put in numerical terms it can be seen that a real good had been achieved by them.

The growth in population created many problems and ensured that the life of the people of Liverpool was changing rapidly at this time. Physically, the town was expanding and the former open areas within the boundaries were being covered by streets of new housing. For many years the expansion of the town had been inhibited by the fact that new building to the north was restricted by the Town Fields, to the south areas across the Pool, then known as Harrington and now as Toxteth, these were in the ownership of the Earls of Sefton, as had been areas of the Great Heath to the east of the town. The Earls had opposed widespread building but the Heath had been acquired from them by the Corporation in the late seventeenth century. The Town Fields had originally been agricultural land farmed by the burgesses as open fields. These had been enclosed in the early eighteenth century and developed in a piecemeal fashion with a motley collection of cultivated land, small housing developments, brick fields and pits, all in private ownership. A watercolour sketch by Chubbard in the collection of the Athenaeum clearly shows how the north end of the town was taken up by brick works to provide for the new building of the ever-expanding town. A glass works, mills, Muspratt's chemical works and several rope walks were located in the area.

In October 1774 part of the Town Field area became the terminal basin of the Leeds and Liverpool Canal. This had a marked influence on the establishment of commerce and industry in the surrounding area. The branch at Leeds Street was surrounded by warehouses, coal yards and the unsavoury 'manure yard' from where the night soil and rubbish of Liverpool was transported to fertilise fields along the canal route through Lancashire. To serve these new developments the former Pinfold Lane was widened and paved as Vauxhall Road. What had been a genteel residential area now deteriorated into overcrowded tenements and slums.

Another area ripe for development was the land adjacent to the Moss near the summit of Brownlow Hill and Martindale Hill or Mount Pleasant, as it was known, extending from Parliament Street to Myrtle Street and eastward to Crown Street. The land had been purchased by the Trustees of the Anne Molyneux Charity in 1727 and provided the income which sustained their almshouse that stood at the corner of Hanover Street. The association between the parish churches of Liverpool and the Charity caused this area to be known as the Rector's Fields. The poor in the adjacent workhouse were required to earn their relief by work in cultivating this land. The Special Vestry meeting of 30 October 1823 made it clear that in every case the Vestry had been alert to

require, from the parties seeking relief, an equivalent, in every case where it has been practicable, in the shape of labour -thus throwing them upon their own resources- has had its full share of influence in producing salutary effects. In pursuance of this policy, the Special Vestry have continued to furnish employment to such as from bodily infirmity or from other causes, were not able to procure a more profitable occupation in cultivating the Rector's Fields and in breaking stones for the use of the highways.

In 1801 an agreement was reached to allow the development of this area, in which several of the important builders and architects of the town were involved, including John Foster and Charles Eyes, the cartographer. Little was done for fifteen years when the fields were soon built up with middle-class housing, now largely subsumed or covered by the buildings of the University of Liverpool. These dwellings probably gained in prestige from their proximity to the imposing developments in Abercromby and Faulkner Squares, both of which were being built between 1820 and 1830. This new housing to the south and east of the town was of a high quality and designed to provide accommodation for the wealthy man of business whose social aspirations dictated a move into premises more distant from his counting house than had been customary. Previously, it was common practice for dwelling, workshop and warehouse to be in close proximity or combined into a single group of buildings. Good examples of this sort of arrangement can be seen in the former Royal Institution building in Colquitt Street. This house, built c.1799 for Thomas Parr, has conjoined pavilions, originally a counting house or office and a coach house. At the rear is a large five-storey warehouse. A similar arrangement was used at 129 Dale Street, where the elegant façade of the house is well preserved in Trueman Street. When this house was built, the spirit distillery of its owner, Mr John Houghton, filled the adjacent plot at the rear. This hugger-mugger mixture of housing and workshops, marked by furnace chimneys and shops, is evident in many of Brierley's drawings.

For slightly less wealthy householders, terraces of refined and sophisticated design began to be built. The terrace had been little used in Liverpool prior to this period but now along Duke Street (where Mornington Terrace is a good example), Canning Street, Percy Street, and in the other thoroughfares of that area, they became a common form of housing design. The terrace, as well as affording economies in building costs, allowed the designer to create what looked like large country houses, but subtly divided into a number of units for multiple occupancy. Perhaps the best example is Gambier Terrace, a project financed by the property developer Ambrose Lace, in 1828. The architect is unknown but the grandeur of the original design is breathtaking, with its long, Ionic colonnade terminated at the northern end by a pavilion with massive, attached, Ionic columns. Unfortunately, the design was only partly realised during building in the 1830s and the terrace was completed in the 1870s, using yellow brick in the style of a French chateau. The span of the façade of numbers 3 to 17 in Percy Street gives an idea of the majestic appearance which might have been achieved had the original project for Gambier Terrace been completed.

An indication of the expansion of the town and the way in which new streets of houses were springing up almost overnight is to be found in the order of the Council in 1807 that Roger Phillips was to be authorised to paint the number of each house on the door and to paint the name of every street on the corner buildings. This does not seem to have been done, or, at least, not completed, as in 1820 the following resolution was made: 'Resolved that the names of the several streets throughout the town be painted therein, and the number of the houses be also painted on the doors of the same, under the direction of the Surveyor agreeable to the clause in the Act of Parliament of the 26th of the late King.' The street names painted on the buildings are very evident in many of the Brierley pictures, though house numbers are not apparent. It would seem that the main reason for the introduction of house numbering was to facilitate the collection of the several local rates. In the town centre, the area of Brierley's activities, a very different sort of change from the suburban residential development was occurring. Around the old town's nucleus, marked by the original seven streets – Dale Street, Water Street, Tithebarn Street, Chapel Street, Castle Street, Old Hall Street, and High Street – two things were happening. The working-class housing was confined to the streets and alleys which led off these main thoroughfares, often following the outlines of the burgage plots, hence names such as Hackins Hey and Lancelot Hey (hey being the Lancashire dialect word for a hedge). An idea of the type of housing can be seen in the rare survival in Hockenhall Alley off Dale Street. It is a single bay, brick-built house of the poorest quality, dating from the first decade of the nineteenth century.

Additionally, the former enclosed gardens on the burgage plots had been in-filled by this time with small, crowded courts and warehouses. The 'court', though not peculiar to Liverpool, became a very usual form of accommodation. A series of small cottages was built around a central, paved, open space, which also contained the communal lavatories and a pump for water supply. These courts were usually deficient in drainage and sanitation and were often ill-ventilated and polluted. In 1839 it was calculated that some 35–40,000 people lived in the courts of Liverpool; a figure which had risen to 80,000 by 1848. Many of the new arrivals in Liverpool found a home in the numerous cellars of larger properties which had been abandoned by their previous owners and turned into tenements. They were described thus in 1834: 'The cellars are ten or twelve feet square; generally flagged – but frequently having only the bare earth for a floor, and sometimes less than six feet in height. There is frequently no window so that light and air can gain access to the cellars only by the door, the top of which is often not higher than the level of the street… There is sometimes a back cellar, used as a sleeping apartment, having no direct communication with the external atmosphere, and deriving its scanty supply of light and air solely from the first apartment.' Epidemic disease flourished and the cholera outbreak of 1832 provoked riots. Between 29 May and 10 June there were eight major disturbances and a number of smaller incidents of unrest. The protestors directed their ire mainly at the medical fraternity, accusing the doctors of using the corpses of cholera victims for medical dissection and demanding that they 'Bring out the Burkers', a reference to the case of Burke and Hare of four years earlier. This state of affairs led to the Corporation's decision on 1 January 1847 to appoint Dr William Duncan (Athenaeum Proprietor No. 380) as Britain's first Medical Officer of Health, charged with the improvement of the sanitary condition of the town. The appointment of Duncan was part of a programme in which the Corporation began a series of enlightened improvements to the condition of the poor of Liverpool.

Working-class housing in the old town was coming under increasing pressure when that area began to develop as the business and commercial district. The building of the new Exchange between 1803 and 1808 had created a focus for commercial transactions which had been lacking since the building of the Town Hall in 1754. In that building, the design of John Woods had included a central court to serve as a place for conducting business. This proved inadequate and was later enclosed and glazed to provide administrative premises. The place of business tended to be on the open space at the rear of the building, which was eventually paved, after prolonged disputes about the merits of paving and cobbling, and became known as 'Exchange Flags'. At first, some of the paving stones were not properly set and wobbled when walked upon – a particular annoyance to the well-dressed business men who complained that jets of muddy water soiled their white trousers. The Exchange Building was a speculative venture, financed not by the civic authorities but by the business community. The architect of the threesided courtyard was the ubiquitous John Foster Senior. Such was the popularity and success of this commercial development that it acted as a magnet to business houses, whose proprietors conducted their deals face to face. Convenience dictated that businesses were drawn to the streets and properties within easy walking distance of the Exchange, displacing former residences and retail enterprises. Brierley's drawings are very valuable in capturing the appearance of the town centre when it was still a medley of houses, workshops, retailers and beer houses, before the old streets and buildings were swept away to be replaced by counting houses, offices and warehouses, together with shops, taverns and eating houses. The pressures that the growing physical extent of the town, the number of buildings and the enlarged population placed on the civic administration were numerous. The people had to be fed, the streets cleaned, paved and lit, the links of transport had to be improved to ensure distribution of food supplies and the easy transportation of goods to and from the port, where new docks and enlarged facilities were required. The sick needed care, the infirm and handicapped had to be relieved, provision made for the poor and needy, the improvement of water supply and sanitation was essential and the town had to be policed and made safe from fire.

The responsibility for dealing with these problems lay principally with two bodies. The first of these was the Corporation or Council of the Borough. The powers of this body, presided over by the Mayor, were based on the Royal Charters of the town which constituted its borough status. The Royal Charter of William III in 1695 resulted in the transference of civic power from the Freemen and burgesses into the hands of a narrow mercantile elite. The Council was to consist 'of forty and one honest and discreet men of the burgesses of the town'. In the new charter, deliberately or not, no provision was made for the selection of the Common Councilmen. They assumed the right to select their own membership, which became an oligarchic group of the most important families, principally drawn from the mercantile and commercial elite, who were Tory in their politics and Anglican in their religious inclinations, rather than the craftsmen and tradesmen who had been in power previously. Consequently, the government of Liverpool was uniquely in the hands of the wealthy, self-perpetuating oligarchs of the mercantile elite. The responsibilities of the Corporation were concentrated on the physical growth of the town, the extension of the dock estate and the creation of wealth.

The period was not without controversial topics when the Corporation might be expected to represent the views of the townspeople. Amongst the major issues of the period, which was supported by the more liberal Tories, was the campaign for repeal of the Corn Laws. The attempt to control and limit the import of foreign grain in order to protect English growers had a particular resonance with the influential corn merchants of Liverpool. The campaign for abolition seems to have met with a mixed response. In April 1825 William Huskisson, one of the town's Members of Parliament, a warm and passionate advocate of the abolition of the Corn Laws, sponsored a Bill to that effect. The Corn Laws were eventually repealed in 1846 after prolonged and often bitter campaigning by one of the first national, organised, lobbying and protest organisations – the Anti-Corn-Law League.

Another issue which provoked strong emotion was the discussion begun in 1825 on proposals to repeal the penal laws against Roman Catholics. These restrictions, which dated from the religious conflicts of the sixteenth and seventeenth centuries, had been gradually falling into desuetude and had been much eased by the Catholic Relief Acts dating from 1778 to 1793. The first Act had provoked such violence in the Gordon Riots (1780) that progress was slow in removing the remaining restrictions. In Liverpool, there was a sharp division of opinion. Though the population was predominantly Protestant, the presence of a large Irish immigrant population and the strong Roman Catholic element in the people of the hinterland made Liverpool liable to religious factions.

The Council was much preoccupied with the expansion of the dock system. Contrary to the worst fears of the 'Guinea Men', the abolition of the slave trade in 1807 had not brought about the total collapse of Liverpool's commerce. On the contrary, there was a steady increase in other mercantile activities to compensate for the loss of the 'Africa Trade'. That it left a legacy is confirmed by the directories of the period which show that Liverpool in 1824 had two dealers in 'Negro clothing' and one dealer in 'Plantation tools'. Most of the ships using the port for ocean trading in the 1820s were on the traditional Liverpool routes to North and South America, the West Indies and Africa.

They carried out from the shores of Britain manufactured goods of all types. So diverse were the cargoes of the ships that the Customs Service used the term 'Liverpool goods' as a category of mixed cargo. The returning ships brought back the traditional imports of cotton, sugar, tobacco and various other exotic woods and dyestuffs. The links with Africa, forged by the 'Guinea Men' of the previous century, were still in use, supplying the West African coast with cotton cloth, ironware and various other trade goods. Ships sailed from Liverpool to the Mediterranean and the Levant. Traffic to and from India and the Far East was largely closed to merchants at this time due to the monopoly enjoyed by the Honourable East India Company, which used a route that would eventually become a vital component of the trade of Liverpool.

Two other areas of maritime activity are easily overlooked. The first of these was the rapidly increasing passenger trade, carrying emigrants to the New World, especially after the introduction of steam packets in 1840. Though the packet ships were seen as glamorous, perhaps more economically significant to the wealth of Liverpool was the myriad of coastal sloops and schooners that carried load after load of mundane goods and passengers around the whole coast of the British Isles, mainly from the basin of the Old Dock where they lay with destination boards in their rigging. These were the HGVs of the period and, though mainly directed to Ireland, there were regular services to all parts of the British Isles [see Liverpool 800 ed. Belchem, LUP 2007 p.183].

Essential to the ever-growing trade of Liverpool was the dock system. The original anchorage for the port had been the area of the river fronting the town. There, ships were beached either to discharge or take on cargo. If this was not possible, they lay further out in the Sloyne near Rock Ferry or the Hoyle Lake off the northern end of the Wirral Peninsula and used lighters with all the expense and risk of loading and unloading their burdens. The first dock – known as the Old Dock – opened in 1715 and had obviated the difficulties of these practices and allowed ships to be worked regardless of the state of the tide. Recent excavations during the construction of the Liverpool One shopping area uncovered the buried remains of most of the

Old Dock which is now open to visitors. The success of the Old Dock was such that by 1820 four more docks had been built and plans for further expansion were well advanced. In addition to these major docks a number of smaller basins intended for use by canal and river boats had been built by the inland navigation companies, the most important being Duke's Dock, opened in 1773, and the Manchester and Chester Basins of 1785–90. During recent work on the site of the new Museum of Liverpool Life the basin of the Manchester Dock, abandoned in the mid-1920s, was unearthed in a remarkable state of preservation. These comparatively small canal docks were overshadowed by the much grander scheme to add two new, large docks on the south end of the system. Much of this extension work was supervised by John Foster Senior. It has been calculated that the work he directed doubled the dock space available in the port. Despite the enlargement of the docks

View of the Old Dock.

they were still proving inadequate to meet the ever-increasing demand. By 1824 the number of vessels entering and leaving the port had risen to 10,000, with a total tonnage of 1,180,914. The introduction of steam ships required new elements in the design of docks. Experiments with steam vessels had been made since 1815 but the engines were still regarded as too unreliable for ocean voyages until on 20 June 1818 the town was aroused by the arrival of the steam ship Savannah under the command of Captain Rogers, which had used steam power for at least some of its voyage from the eponymous Georgia port.

The business of managing both the town and the docks was proving too much for the Corporation. However, the Dock Act of 1825 not only gave consent to the expansion of the dock system but also established the Dock Committee, thus theoretically separating the functions of the Corporation and the management of the docks, though the personnel of the two organisations was identical. Under the provision of the previous Act of 1811, expansion had been continued by the construction of Prince's Dock, begun in 1816, under the direction of John Foster. It was completed in 1821. Brunswick Dock at the south end of the system was the first to be built in response to the 1825 Act and when opened in 1832, it was the largest and most commodious dock in the port. A decision was now made after much discussion and consultation with eminent engineers, notably John Rennie and William Jessop, that further expansion should take place at the northern end of the system and this resulted in the building of Clarence Dock, opened in May 1830, and in the succeeding years Waterloo, Victoria and Trafalgar Docks were opened by 1836. After 1824, Foster left his post as Dock Surveyor and was succeeded by the great Jesse Hartley who held the post for the next thirty-six years.

Foster has been mentioned several times. He was a colossus who bestrode Liverpool in the first decades of the nineteenth century and his rise and unexpected and largely unexplained fall must have been a constant source of conversation for Brierley and his contemporaries. John Foster, the son of a Master Joiner, was born in Liverpool in 1759. His activities and the way in which he insinuated members of his family into key civic posts has led one recent writer to remark, 'Foster was master, and sometimes inventor, of almost every known form of local government corruption'. After being apprenticed to his father, John quickly established a local reputation as an architect. He prepared the plans for the new gaol, the Athenaeum, the Exchange, the Town Hall and the extension for the Theatre Royal, as well as designs for St Luke's Church, St Martin-in-the-Fields, St Andrew's in Rodney Street and numerous other landmark buildings; for example, the new Infirmary. He was able to establish himself in a position of great civic influence and earn a reputation for town planning and street improvement, as well as laying down the rules for building regulations in the town. It must be said that many in Liverpool regarded his business activities and methods as dubious. Appointed as Dock Surveyor in 1802, he was given additional duties when he was also made Surveyor to the Corporation, a post which gave him responsibility for both town planning and the design of civic buildings. In his duties as Dock Surveyor Foster was not idle. He was able to extend and enlarge the area of the docks by more than twenty acres despite the decision to close and fill in the Old Dock, which was now inconvenient, small and obsolescent.

The last major work undertaken by John Foster the Elder was the building of the new Prince's Dock which was intended to be of greater size than its predecessors and to offer improved facilities. This scheme for the northward expansion of the dock system had been given Parliamentary approval in 1799. The dock was opened on 19 June 1821 to coincide with the Coronation Day of George IV, the expectation of the Corporation being that the ceremony would contribute to 'the further entertainment of various classes of tradesmen and societies'. The day may have been enlivened by the procession in which the glass makers wore glass hats decorated with feathers of the same material and each man with a glass sword; the potters from Herculaneum paraded examples of their work; while the Company of Whalers trundled an Eskimo canoe fitted with wheels. Despite the revelry, dark shadows loomed over John Foster as the West Indiaman Mary, the steamer Majestic and the American ship Martha made their way into the dock.

The delay in completion of the dock may have been partly due to the years of warfare and the economic strictures of the time, but most people suspected a darker reason. There were rumours, scandalous gossip and accusations to explain why the building of this dock seemed to be a bottomless pit that absorbed money almost faster than it could be raised. In 1822, the new Audit Commission, largely made up of men who were not part of the charmed circle of the Corporation and Dock Committee, reported that they had found abundant evidence of overcharging for materials and a failure to regulate supply.

As the net closed, a new assistant was appointed to Foster. Jesse Hartley took up his position on 24 March 1824, having previously served in West Yorkshire, Ireland and as Bridge Master of the Salford Hundred. Three days later John Foster sent a letter to the Corporation offering his resignation. It offered no reasons, excuses or explanations and was accepted by the Council without thanks or acknowledgement or note of regret. Without any recognition, Foster left office to go into a prosperous retirement in Westmorland. On his death, Foster was possessed of an estate of £60,000 and considerable property in that county and Liverpool ['The Interests and Ethics of John Foster Dock Surveyor 1799–1824', Jarvis A., THSLC. vol. 140, 1991]. Jesse Hartley assumed the position of Dock Surveyor and was to become the moving genius behind the huge expansion of the dock system.

While the Council took responsibility for international, national and local matters of development, much of the onus for the domestic, social and welfare administration of Liverpool lay in the hands of the Vestry. This body of a dozen or so men, headed by the churchwardens, was a development of the Elizabethan system of local government in which the organisation of Poor Relief, the cleanliness and repair of the streets and the maintenance of law and order were placed in the hands of locally chosen, voluntary officers. These officials were selected by popular vote at a public meeting, or 'Open Vestry', held in the parish church at Easter in which all adult males had a right to vote. As the extent of legislation had grown and as the financial responsibility for the collection and disbursement of money raised on local rates increased, it was

found that the responsibilities for day-to-day administration were too great for a part-time, possibly reluctant 'volunteer' group, and so a complement of full-time, paid officials was engaged to assist with the duties. Designed to operate in rural parishes with small populations, the Open Vestry system began to fail in urban parishes, and from the seventeenth century onwards there were 'Select Vestries', a self-perpetuating body of residents responsible for the civic management of the parish, created either by Act of Parliament or by Bishop's Faculty. This did not happen in Liverpool until 1820 when a Select Vestry for Liverpool was officially established. Prior to this, affairs in the town had largely been conducted by a self-electing committee of twenty, formed from the General Vestry who, from the middle of the eighteenth century, had undertaken the management of the town.

premises on Brownlow Hill. Associated with the Infirmary was the Sailors' Hospital of 1752 which occupied wings of the Infirmary building and after 1824 was financed by deductions from the pay of sailors. The Dispensary on Church Street was established in 1778, and in association with various private charities the parish provided a midwifery service. The Vestry also undertook the maintenance of the prisons, shared in the construction and manning of the defences of the Mersey, and from 1747 had a fire and police service for Liverpool.

A crowded town with many warehouses packed with highly inflammable goods made fire an ever-present, serious danger in Liverpool. The danger was exemplified on 28 August 1825, when four ship-building yards and two vessels on the slipways, a steam boat and a ship of 400 tons were consumed by fire at a cost estimated at £25,000. In 1826, the Vestry undertook the setting up of the first regular fire brigade in Liverpool.

The role of Constable had always been associated with a Vestry official and now, by 1748, a force of sixty watchmen, scavengers and street cleaners was set up in Liverpool. The town was divided into nine districts each of which had two watchmen, their work being supervised by a local commissioner. Additionally, a separate force of Dock Watchmen protected the lands of the dock estate. It was not until 1836 that the various law enforcement agencies were combined into a single force on the model of the London Metropolitan Service. The force was not short of employment in a town where the natural portion of the criminally inclined was supplemented by sailors' doxies, pimps, crimps, and sailor men with money in their pockets and little time to spend it. To this multinational melting pot were added the conflicts of religious disputes and political differences, most of which it was felt could be reconciled by physical violence. In his novel Redburn of 1839 Herman Melville writes of the Liverpool waterfront: '… of all the seaports in the world, Liverpool, perhaps, most abounds in all the variety of land-sharks, land-rats, and other vermin, which makes the hapless mariner their prey. In the shape of landlords, bar-keepers, clothiers, crimps, and boarding-house loungers, the landsharks devour him, limb by limb; while the land-rats and mice constantly nibble at his purse.'

Edward Blackstock
A lawyer with chambers in Water Street, Blackstock was for many years the solicitor and Clerk to the Vestry, a post which carried no salary but provided an annual income of more than £1,000 in fees during the course of a year.

Dominated by the churchwardens, the Committee (often confusingly referred to by themselves as 'The Select Vestry') not only managed the increasingly complicated Poor Law and the care of the churches but had undertaken the provision of hospitals. The Infirmary had been opened in 1749, partly funded by the parish and partly by private charity, and in 1824 was removed into new

However, it was not only this petty crime with which the police agents had to contend. In 1826 the townspeople were horrified by an event which started at the docks but eventually led to investigations in fashionable Hope Street. Three barrels containing corpses preserved in salt were discovered on board the Glasgow steam packet. When the case was investigated the carter who had brought the barrels to the ship reported that the load originated in a cellar in Hope Street. On being searched, the house was found to contain a further 33 bodies which had been resurrected from the nearby parish cemetery of St James and were being sold as anatomical specimens.

Another aspect of the responsibilities of the Vestry was the paving and cleansing of the streets. It was in 1799 that the Council, with the approval of the Vestry, petitioned Parliament for an Improvement Act to enable the paving of the streets and the installation of a proper sewerage system. When approval was given, a major improvement of the roads followed. Until this time the street illumination had been provided by scattered lamps burning whale oil. In January 1816 two gas lamps were installed near the Town Hall and a company with works in Dale Street was set up to introduce gas lighting throughout the town but little was done for some time. Despite the paving and the widening of many streets, the problem of cleanliness was not immediately solved and, as late as 1829, the Vestry meeting registered its dissatisfaction: 'It is the opinion of this Vestry that the inhabitants of this parish suffer great inconvenience from the imperfect sewerage of the town and it is thought highly desirable to remedy the same.'

A major part of the responsibilities of the Vestry was the distribution of Poor Relief and the running and supervision of the workhouse. The Poor Rate was set and collected by the Vestry, under the supervision of the Overseer. In Liverpool, the selected Overseer held an honorary post and was assisted by three stipendiary officers. In 1821, these were Anthony Black, John Aldersey and George Forewood, together with a Workhouse Governor, William Hardman, and the Treasurer, William Dickson. Some idea of the intensity of their work can be gathered from the fact that a weekly meeting was held and a representative of the Committee could be found daily at St Peter's Church ready to deal with urgent cases.

Early nineteenth-century administrators of the Poor Relief found themselves in something of a dilemma. In general, they wished, conscientiously, to relieve need in a decent and humane way – the days of the dread of the Poor Law were to come after the Amendment Act of 1834. At the same time, their continued employment in office might very well rest on the economy with which they spent the Poor Rate levied on all householders. In May 1822, to make provision for medical care for the poor, it was agreed that the Churchwardens and Overseers '… were to treat with the Committee of the Liverpool Dispensary for medical attendance and the supply of medicines to the sick out-poor of this parish, and that a sum not exceeding £500 be appropriated for this purpose out of the Poor Rates.' The Dispensary was located on the corner of Church Alley, near the Athenaeum. On the other hand, the need to conserve resources is clearly laid out in the report for 1822: 'The Vestry … have kept in view that their authority is a sacred trust, the funds at their disposal are the accumulation of industry, that they are compulsorily levied and that the utmost economy ought to be levied in their management.' One economy measure of this time was the decision to concentrate their various offices and departments in a single building. 'The importance of concentrating public offices must be obvious to everyone; and your Select Vestry congratulate the Parish that this desideratum will very shortly be attained, the Churchwardens and Overseers having agreed with the Corporation for the spacious and very convenient premises in Water Street [late the King's Arms] to which not only the respective Boards connected with the Parish, but their officers, constables and servants will be speedily removed; and for the conveniency of the Poor, a large, covered space will be appropriated to them from the inclemency of the weather, during their attendance on the Select Vestry and Overseers.' It was the administration of Poor Relief which takes up the greater part of the discussions of the Vestry and the variety of business raised does much to illuminate the life of those on the outer fringes of Georgian society, far removed from the wealth and luxury that were becoming more and more prevalent amongst the prosperous Liverpool elite (see Peet, Henry ed. The Liverpool Vestry Books Liverpool 1915).

Liverpool's first Poor Houses of 1601 and 1723 had been located near the Pool. A plan to move the Poor House to Brownlow Hill was accomplished in 1770. This building, with later extensions including the House of Correction, was in use in the time of Brierley. The purpose of the House of Correction was to administer a 'short, sharp, shock' to minor offenders, fraudulent Poor Law claimants and often, to unmarried pregnant women.

Mary Ralphson and David Stewart Salmon
The longevity of these two centenarians may be a testament to the humanity of the Poor Law authorities in Liverpool from whom they received 'Outdoor Relief'. Both had had exciting lives; Mary had served in the army alongside her husband and fought at the Battle of Dettingen (1743), while David, after sixty years' service in the Royal Navy, was the last survivor of Anson's voyage around the world (1740–44)

It is obvious that the Liverpool Workhouse, where a stringent economy was practised, was not a place of luxury or one where the inmates were encouraged to take their ease. In the decade of the 1820s, however, there is evidence that a humanitarian spirit prevailed. For example, we find that in April 1826 the Vestry issued an order that 'Henceforth the women in the workhouse of the age of sixty years and upwards shall have allowance of tea, sugar and butter,

and that they, as well as the men, of the age of sixty shall have allowance of tobacco or snuff'. Another indication of the attitude of the Liverpool Poor Law administrators is their firm determination to reject the proposal made in a Bill raised in Parliament in 1823 which was intended to force paupers to wear a badge and to enable magistrates to order the paupers into the militia. There are other signs which indicate a degree of sympathy and compassion that would not be manifest by Poor Law authorities a few years later. Lest it be thought that the Liverpool Poor Law Board was lax, it is evident that the occupants of the workhouse were expected to earn their keep in a variety of activities. The Minutes of the Vestry show that looms were installed and used for the production of calicoes and baizes. The looms were mainly operated by the children who were sufficiently malleable to learn a new skill – it was found that older paupers were best used in breaking stones for the highways and working in the cultivation of the Rector's Fields. It was thought desirable to carry '… this system of labour to its utmost extent, and with a view to induce industrious habits among children of the outdoor poor, by obliging them to contribute in some measure to the support of their necessitous parents'. In 1822, eighty-five children were making textiles while others were employed in the manufacture of pins – though this was found to be unprofitable and abandoned after two years. Many children were apprenticed to tradesmen both in Liverpool and in more distant places. When one considers the dreary stories associated with pauper apprentices it is cheering to learn of 'the liberal practice, long-pursued and still continued of giving each child, when apprenticed out, a double suit of clothing, at considerable expense … the Select Vestry are persuaded that none will grudge the cost for such an object, especially as it assists in obtaining preference among the more respectable manufacturers'. These employments not only provided an income to supplement the Poor Law but also had other effects. 'It is satisfactory to observe that their visible amelioration of manner, their docility and willingness to receive instruction and cheerfulness under restraint offer encouragement.' The poor mites were probably too exhausted to display much childish spirit. The diet of the poor was reviewed from time to time and new kitchens with steam cookers were introduced in 1824; these showed a marked increase in efficiency and economy. In 1826, the rise in the annual cost of the workhouse was partially ascribed to higher numbers of inmates – 1,171 contrasted with 995 in the previous year – and to the rising cost of oatmeal, potatoes and butcher's meat. On another occasion, when it was resolved to discontinue the issue of ale and beer to the able-bodied, it was noted that 'The Select Vestry … from the conviction that the law does not authorise the providing of the Poor with anything beyond a sufficiency of plain, wholesome food.'

It must have been with some relief that the Committee turned to more mundane and trivial matters from the major issues related to the Poor Law. For instance, the proposal of Mr Richardson that a board should be fixed to the Parish Office wall giving the sailing details of the government packets from the port of Liverpool must have been seen as light-hearted and trivial. Strangely, this also had to be referred to the Commissioner of the Watch, Scavengers and Lamps and also to the Surveyor of the Highways!

Not all the inhabitants of Liverpool were seeking Poor Relief. It is obvious that many of those working in Liverpool were either sailors or worked in trades associated with the sea and shipping. However, the employment pattern of the town gives us many insights into life on Merseyside. Official records of employment are few and far between. In the censuses of 1821 and 1831 there is little specific data given and the returns mostly comprise a raw total of occupations divided into arbitrary classes. In the earlier census when the population of the Liverpool township was recorded as 118,972, there were three categories: agriculture; manufacture, commerce and handicrafts; and 'other'. The survey of 1831 which listed a population of 165,175 used the same categories. *

Three categories of principal employment for families in 1821 were listed. Employed in agriculture 131 families; in trade, handicrafts and manufacture a further 11,481 families and in the 'Other' category 13,758. Toxteth Park was enumerated separately and had 34 families engaged in agriculture, 991 in trade etc., with 1555 in 'Other' occupations. In 1831, the figures for Liverpool are 126 in agriculture, 16,967 in trades and manufacturing and 16,085 in the portmanteau group of 'Other'. At the same date, Toxtexth Park had 101 in agriculture, 1914 in trades and manufacture, while a further 2929 families were in other occupations. Data supplied by University of Essex UK data archive.

To supplement this raw data, use can be made of the directories which appeared annually. Especially helpful, although it cannot be regarded as definitive, is the list of occupations included in Baines' Directory of Lancashire, 1825. This lists no fewer than 254 occupations with names and addresses. The catalogue starts with the 307 boarding and day academies, and schools. The presence of so many places of learning contradicts the usual view that opportunities for education and the acquisition of literacy were scarce. Baines' list ends with the three worsted warehouses. Between these two extremes the scope is huge. The different types of employments recorded range from the single dealer in hair plaster to the four ginger beer manufacturers, the four truss makers – hernia being one of the most common injuries suffered by seafarers – and seven dentists. Though such a multiplicity of trades is evident, the list also shows a strong inclination to trades associated with the sea or which have a maritime connection: boat builders, shipping brokers, coopers, ships' chandlers, gunpowder mills, herring merchants, marine store dealers, mast block and pump makers, saw mills and yards, rope makers and shipwrights.

The variety of trades and occupations seems almost dizzying when compared with Liverpool today and reflects the period when an urban area was a self-sustaining and self-sufficient community. One of the effects of the railway revolution of the nineteenth century was that it allowed the concentration of manufacture in those areas where local conditions and supplies of fuel, raw materials and skilled labour were readily available. The railways provided a swift and cheap method of circulation, local specialities could be distributed and it was no longer necessary for towns and regions to provide for all their wants. A good example is the decline of the Liverpool pottery industry. Throughout the eighteenth-century Liverpool and Prescot had developed the manufacture of coarse earthenware. The process was refined and by the second half of the century potteries in Liverpool were producing fine earthenware and porcelain which was widely distributed in the town and exported. However, competition from the large, industrial Staffordshire potteries quickly drove them out of business after the advent of rail and canal transport and by 1841 even the celebrated Herculaneum Pottery had closed.

This then was the environment in which James Brierley lived and worked during his productive decade. It was a town of contrast and paradox. In Liverpool, great wealth – perhaps the most prosperous commercial aristocracy outside the City of London – rubbed shoulders with an enormous population of the very poor. It was a place where the wealthy lived in splendid houses, designed in the latest architectural fashion, while others lived in cellars and courts in the most abject conditions. It was a town which had what was probably the largest workhouse in England and rural mansions of aristocratic style; a town where cultured men and women enjoyed theatre, arts and music; while others lived in a squalid alcoholic haze in the beer shops and stews of the waterfront. It was a place where the wealthy enjoyed every amenity but the streets were often filthy and unpaved. The buildings of Liverpool were an hodge podge of styles and ages with elegant mansions rubbing shoulders with survivors from former times. Liverpool's population travelled to all corners of the globe or scarcely moved from the cellar or court. It was a town which could welcome the latest in technology – pioneering canals, railways and docks – but which was governed by a Corporation medieval in character and dominated by a self-electing faction. To this day there is an excitement and vitality to be found in the streets of Liverpool – the passers-by are lively and often funny, welcoming and friendly – but at the same time not to be taken for granted or disregarded. Liverpool still shows its two faces. A visit to the quiet, polite and dignified calm of the Athenaeum still comes as a sharp contrast to the hustle, the buskers and the food stalls of Church Street.

Notes on the Portraits

All of these portraits are drawn from the Athenaeum Library's extensive collection, principally of Liverpool and Merseyside personalities. The pencil portraits used here are taken from the Athenaeum's collection of sketches by Thomas Hargreaves (Hargraves), 1774–1847. The son of a draper in Castle Street, he entered the Royal Academy Schools as an apprentice in 1790, possibly on the recommendation of Sir Thomas Lawrence with whom he had served an apprenticeship. He exhibited at the Royal Academy and was a founder of the British Society of Artists. From 1803 he worked in Liverpool, principally as a portrait and miniature painter, with a large practice in Lancashire and Cheshire, and was a founder member of the Liverpool Academy. He had two sons who assisted in the family miniature painting business based in Bold Street. The Athenaeum holds one of the most important collections of Hargreaves' work.

The Athenaeum Library: its history and collections
John Tiernan M.A., F.L.A., former Assistant Director, Central Library, Liverpool

Liverpool has a distinguished history in the provision of libraries – public, private and academic – commencing with the establishment in 1715 of a seamen's library at the Parish Church of St Peter's, through the bequest of £30 'to buy books for the library' from a mariner, John Fell (or Fells). This collection contained many early theological books printed in the sixteenth and seventeenth centuries in Antwerp, Geneva, Cologne, Amsterdam, Louvain, Brussels and Paris. It seems that it was not heavily used, possibly because the books were chained to the book cases, and it is not known when it was dissolved or what happened to its contents. It was presumably still in existence in 1893 when Henry Peet published a catalogue of its contents in 'An inventory of the … Parish churches of Liverpool'.

The first major development in library services was the creation in 1757 of the Liverpool Library by William Everard, a mathematician, schoolmaster and architect who was also its first librarian. Initially, the collection was located in Everard's house in St Paul's Square, but following his dismissal as librarian, and three subsequent moves of premises, it was established in a new building in Bold Street in 1803. This was named the Lyceum following the current fashion for classical allusion and was designed by the eminent architect Thomas Harrison of Chester. The institution was owned by shareholders (or proprietors), one of whom was William Roscoe.

In 1783, a prospectus entitled 'For the Establishment of a Coffee Room, Hotel and Tavern at Liverpool, upon a Tontine Scheme, with the benefit of Survivorship' was issued. This resulted in the establishment, in or around 1785, of a hotel – eventually known as 'Bates' Hotel' – at the junction of Lord Street with Whitechapel. It contained a coffee room and newsroom, the latter supplied with copies of current newspapers and journals. Eventually, this accommodation and that of the Lyceum became too busy for the demands placed upon them and a group of leading Liverpool merchants and professional men proposed the creation of another newsroom in a new building, which would also contain a substantial reference library. Following consultation and public meetings, this institution was founded and named the Athenaeum.

The General Committee of the Institution moved swiftly to engage staff and in 1798 the post of Librarian was created, although in advance of an appointment the purchase of books worth £2,013 was agreed, following consultation with 'eminent scholars throughout the country'; for example, Sir Joseph Banks advised on the choice of natural history books and several clergymen selected titles relating to theology, ethics and metaphysics. Books on Greek and Roman classics and works in modern European languages were selected by a sub-committee consisting of founder Proprietors Roscoe, Drs James Currie and John Rutter.

Thus the initial collection comprised books 'which no gentleman's library should be without', and included the Statutes at Large; the Gentleman's Magazine; the Annual Register and the transactions of various learned societies; while the Parish of Liverpool deposited the manuscript return of the 1801 census, one of the few such complete returns known in England and a fascinating contemporary picture of the town's population. In 1800 the Corporation of Liverpool presented the Atlantic Neptune – two large folio volumes of marine charts of the North American coast, published for the use of the Royal Navy. According to Frederick Blair, writing in 1947, no two identical copies of this work are known. In view of Liverpool's rapidly growing mercantile trade another important early addition to the library's stock was Captain Greenville Collins' Great Britain's Coasting Pilot, a pioneering survey of the entire coast of Great Britain, published in 1693. London and provincial newspapers were also purchased for use in the newsroom. In 1802 the first printed catalogue of the library which contained entries for over 6,000 volumes was published. This was followed by another in 1820 when over 10,000 volumes were recorded, and then by the catalogue of 1864 with over 20,000 volumes.

In 1799, following another selection of purchases by the committee, the first Librarian, William Gearing, was 'elected'. Gearing, although given explicit instructions as to his duties, was soon in trouble, because, in 1800, the committee recorded that he 'shall not be allowed the use of spirits in the

Athenaeum, and that the President is requested to remonstrate with him upon the impropriety of his behaviour'. He must, however, have overcome this initial setback because when he retired at the age of eighty in 1817, the committee agreed that, due to his faithful service, his salary of sixty guineas should continue to be paid for the rest of his life and that he should also be granted free access to the library and newsroom. In 1800, J. R. Davis was appointed Assistant Librarian at £25 per annum, but in 1802 he was accused of theft and dismissed. An inspection of the library's stock was ordered in the wake of this, so it seems likely that he was stealing from the collections.

From its establishment, the Athenaeum's membership represented a liberal diversity of religious viewpoints. Its earliest members included many Unitarians – many of the town's merchants, including Roscoe, were adherents of the denomination – and other Non-conformists, as well as Anglicans. There were also Jewish Proprietors who presented some valuable Hebrew artefacts to the institution, as well as Fr Jean Baptiste Gerardot, a French Roman Catholic émigré, founder of the church of St Anthony, Scotland Road, who was a refugee from the anti-clerical revolution in his native land. Another notable cleric, who presented a large number of Spanish theological works to the library, was Joseph Blanco White – himself a Spaniard (although born of an Irish family) – who started his ministry as a Catholic priest, then became an Anglican parson and ended his checkered ecclesiastical career as a Unitarian minister.

Roscoe was a man of liberal mind. He was, for example, opposed to the slave trade and in favour of American Independence and the French Revolution. As a patron of the arts he came to the aid of John James Audubon (the American artist and author of The Birds of America), and supported his endeavours when he visited Liverpool seeking patronage. Roscoe was particularly helpful to a young refugee from political persecution in Italy, Antonio Panizzi, whom he housed and for whom he obtained local employment as a teacher of Italian. Panizzi eventually moved to London, where he lectured in Italian at University College and was subsequently appointed as an assistant librarian at the British Museum, eventually becoming Director and Librarian of that institution and ending his days as Sir Anthony Panizzi: 'Prince of Librarians' and an Italian senator.

By 1805 the Athenaeum was experiencing financial difficulties, probably due to the unstable economic and political situation in Europe, and as the institution was in debt to the tune of £200, the purchase of books was restricted. By 1811 events took a turn for the worse when the Athenaeum's bankers, Clarke and Roscoe, owed the institution £460, and the services of the bank were terminated. The bank's eventual failure led to the personal bankruptcy, in 1815, of William Roscoe, one of its partners, and the eminent bibliophile and collector of Renaissance Italian art was forced to sell his books and pictures by auction – ironically by the auctioneer Thomas Winstanley, whose premises were adjacent to the Athenaeum. A number of Roscoe's friends attended the auction of his library and bid for and obtained a considerable number of books, so that, in 1817, the committee recorded 'the gift of Mr William Rathbone and others of most of William Roscoe's library' with the wish that they should be made easily accessible for his lifetime. The grateful recipient of this generosity later thanked the committee and made further gifts to the Athenaeum. The Roscoe collection is housed in a fine glazed bookcase, and its contents include the manuscript (in four large volumes) of Roscoe's The Life and Pontificate of Leo the Tenth, as well as many important works relating to Renaissance Italian art and culture. One of many other interesting items in the collection is King Henry VIII's Assertio Septem Sacramentorum adversus Martin Luther, published by the king's printer, Richard Pynson, in 1521. This was the work which gained the monarch the title Defender of the Faith, granted by Pope Leo X. Examples in the collection of Roscoe's great interest in botany are his Monandrian Plants (published in parts between 1824 and 1828) and the work of Mrs Edward (Priscilla) Bury, who had been encouraged by Roscoe to produce her Hexandrian Plants (eventually published between 1831 and 1837).

Following a pioneering start, the library continued to grow in strength during the nineteenth century. To the usual 'gentlemen's library' subjects of theology, history, topography and travel, biography, science and the liberal arts, were added many important collections, either by purchase or through the generosity of individual Proprietors. Manuscript items include examples of Persian and Jewish documents and a handwritten version of Cicero's Orations, prepared in 1499. As well as printed books, maps, drawings and portraits, local items were also regularly purchased for the library's stock. Drawings and prints include the Brierley and Hargreaves collections, and a series of original caricatures of well-known nineteenth-century Liverpool worthies by Liberio Prosperi, one of Vanity Fair's artists. There is a number of incunabula (early printed books) representing the work of famous pioneers of printing such as Aldus Manutius, Louis Elzevier and Christopher Plantin; a notable example being a beautifully coloured Book of Hours which, although it looks like an illuminated manuscript, is actually printed and dates from 1517. First editions include the only known genuine original copy of Gore's first Directory of Liverpool, published in 1766, and Hannah Glasse's The Art of Cookery (1765) and The Compleate Confectioner (c.1760) – domestic cookery books which predate Mrs Beeton by nearly a century. The library also possesses the first edition (1839) of Bradshaw's Railway Time Tables and Assistant to Railway Travelling. Maps represented in the collection include atlases of England by John Speed and of the world by the Dutch cartographers Johannes Blaeu and Gerardus Mercator, all published in the late sixteenth and early seventeenth centuries. Moving forward to the early eighteenth and the nineteenth centuries, the map collection includes fine examples of early surveys of Liverpool from 1725 onwards and the first edition of the Ordnance Survey, 1832–1853, as well as the six inch to the mile first edition of 1844–1849 and the five feet to the mile O.S. survey of Liverpool of 1849. Other important local collections include 22 volumes of Liverpool playbills for the period 1773–1830. A multi-volume boxed collection of pamphlets, now fully catalogued for the first time, includes many rare and fugitive items.

As often seems to happen in any library of importance there are several items in stock that were thought shocking to Victorian sensibilities, including an 1895 donation by James Lister, a wealthy Athenaeum Proprietor, of Louis Barré and Henri Roux's Herculanum et Pompei (1875–1877), with the stipulation that volume 8, which contains erotic engravings, should be kept under lock and key! Another example of a notorious addition to stock was an anonymous gift of James Joyce's Ulysses (1923) – a rare item, being one of a limited edition of 2,000 copies printed in Paris on hand-made paper. The committee did, however, occasionally act censoriously, as when in 1892 it rejected the purchase of Wynwood Reade's Martyrdom of Man because of its author's unconcealed atheism, and – in the following year – Sir Richard Burton's frank translation of the Arabian Nights' Entertainment (1885–1886) was also turned down. In 1955, a copy of the limited unexpurgated edition of T. E. Lawrence's The Mint, renowned at the time for containing much 'barrack room' language, was acquired without any protest as to its suitability. This was a sign of twentieth century liberality and relaxation towards controversial literature. Later in the century, thanks to their importation and donation by Proprietors, Peter Wright's Spycatcher (1987) and Kitty Kelley's The Royals (1997), both blocked by the courts for publication in the UK, were placed in the library.

Until the twentieth century, the library's collection could only be consulted on the premises, so from 1857 to 1937, the Athenaeum subscribed to Mudie's Circulating Library, which made books for loan to Proprietors available on a rotational basis.

Although the Athenaeum's governing committee was all-powerful at first in terms of book selection and treated the librarian more as a servant than a professional man, the growth of librarianship as a distinct profession in the mid-nineteenth century meant that those holding the post from the 1840s onwards gained more standing in the eyes of the institution. This enhanced status was probably not harmed by the involvement in its management of Sir James Allanson Picton, a Proprietor (and President of the Library Association of the United Kingdom in 1883 and of the Athenaeum itself in 1886) who was also, for nearly forty years, the Chairman of the Liverpool Corporation's Libraries, Museums and Arts Committee.

Sir J. A. Picton 1805–89
Born in Liverpool James Picton, an architect by profession, was a man of
great influence in local affairs. A strong protagonist of the public library
movement, he was instrumental in the establishment of Liverpool's first
public library. Picton was a very active historian, writing voluminously
about the history of the town and, especially, its government.
[Athenaeum Proprietor No. 70]

The appropriately named William Roscoe Jones, who, after ten years' service as assistant to the Librarian, was appointed Master and Librarian in 1841, was, on his retirement in 1885 after 56 years' service in the library, made an honorary member and voted £125 per year for life. His sub-librarian, appointed in 1869, was an Italian, Eugenio Londini, who, in 1881, left the Athenaeum's service to become the first Registrar, Librarian and Lecturer in Italian of the newly established Liverpool University College (later to become the University of Liverpool). In 1891 Londini was made a Knight of the Crown of Italy by King Umberto I. George Thomas Shaw, who was elected Master and Librarian in 1889, having commenced work in the library in 1878 at the age of 14, was appointed Chief Librarian of the City of Liverpool in 1909, where he introduced many innovations to that library service's procedures. The last full-time Master and Librarian was Frederick Blair, who served from 1923–57. Both Shaw's and Blair's professional endeavours were recognised by the award of Honorary MAs from the University of Liverpool. Following Blair's retirement the management of the library was operated through the good offices of an Honorary Librarian, Dr George Chandler (the City Librarian), an Athenaeum Proprietor, who provided staff on a rota basis from the Liverpool Central Library to carry out the Athenaeum library's functions. This arrangement ceased in the early 1970s, and professional cover, with a lapse of some years, has been provided since then by a number of highly qualified retired professional librarians, acting as joint custodians on a part-time basis.

For most of the twentieth century and up to the present day, the Athenaeum has suffered from occasional financial difficulties which have led to restrictions on stock acquisition and, occasionally, to painful and controversial decisions to sell items from the library's stock, in order to ensure the institution's survival. The Athenaeum is the last remaining example in Liverpool of a 'gentlemen's club', others, such as the Lyceum, having been wound up because of lack of income.

The library is still a proud example of the ethos of its founders, and the institution's management has shown continuing faith in its life, by ensuring that its holdings are now being recorded in a computerised catalogue with the ultimate aim of achieving on-line access.

The Athenaeum Library: Further Reading

The principal primary sources are the General Committee Minute Books, commencing in 1797. A scholarly account of the founding of the Library and its early years appears in Frank Gibbons' 'The pre-1850 libraries of Liverpool: their origins, collections, users, and their subsequent history' (unpublished Ph.D. thesis, University of Strathclyde, 1984 – there is a copy of the section relating to the Athenaeum shelved in the Library Office).

Printed sources are: Frederick C. Blair, The Athenaeum Library, Liverpool (1947); Neville Carrick and Edward L. Ashton, The Athenaeum, Liverpool, 1797–1997 (1997); George T. Shaw, History of the Athenaeum, Liverpool, 1797–1898 (1898), and F. Harlan Taylor, Liverpool and the Athenaeum (1965).

James Brierley: the Man and the Artist

Over the period of more than two hundred years that the Athenaeum has been in existence, the institution has gathered many treasures. Amongst these is the collection of ninety ink and watercolour-wash paintings by an obscure local artist, James Brierley, who specialised in the topographical drawings of local buildings and street scenes. These pictures provide the main subject of this book.

The pictures provoke curiosity as to the identity and history of this prolific artist. It is unfortunate that very little information about Brierley is available. Twenty-five years ago, a joint exhibition of his work was arranged with the Liverpool Record Office and the catalogue included a brief biography, in which, unfortunately, no references were given. Examination of this material casts doubts on its accuracy and it seems possible that the researcher confused another family of the same name. In outline, it was suggested that James and Elizabeth Brierley arrived in Liverpool from east Lancashire c.1780. Three sons were born: John in 1782, Thomas in 1786, and James, the subject, in 1791. A baptism date for James at St Nicholas' Church is given as 1 March. Unfortunately, examination of the register of St Nicholas' shows that the father of this child is described as a shipwright, living in Crosbie Street, when we know for certain that the artist was a book-keeper, as will be seen below, or possibly the child of a book-keeper. We also know that there was another Brierley family resident in the town, of which the father was a shipwright, living in the Moorfields area, whose previous children, a girl Ellen and a son Thomas, had been baptised at St Nicholas'. This may be the source of confusion.

James Brierley appears in directories from 1796 when he lived at 21 St James' Street. Another treasure of the Athenaeum is a manuscript book, written by the parish clerks in 1801, recording their findings of the census (the first ever made in Britain), in that year. This is a very significant source which has been little explored by historians (see P. Laxton, A Manuscript Return for the First National Census of Population, THLC, vol. 130, 1981). This includes in Lydian Street [a mis-spelling of Lydia Ann Street] a 'front house' occupied by James Brierley and shared with another family, the total occupants being five males and three females. A 'front house' was one not built to the common 'back to back' design used in so many dwellings for industrial workers at this time. The clerk preparing the census has sometimes described the occupation of the householder but did not do so on this occasion. However, Gore's Directory of 1804 lists James Brierley as a book-keeper, resident at 7 Lydia Ann Street. The census also makes it very clear that their home was in the Parish of St Thomas; it is unfortunate that their registers only exist for the period between 1813 and 1875. The Brierley family removed to Cropper Street by 1805 and remained there until c.1820. Gore's Directory of 1821 has an entry for Brierley, still a book-keeper, but now living at 4 Marquis Street. In the Baines' Directory of 1824/5 James Brierley, Drawing Master, is listed as living at 6 Roscoe Lane. It may be assumed that this is the man who made the drawings for the Athenaeum and was perhaps the son of the original James Brierley, but it is also possible that the retired book-keeper had taken up an old hobby and was now putting it into profitable effect. In a wildly speculative mood it might be suggested that the drawings do not display the exuberance of a young man but the rigid mind and penmanship of an older person who had spent years keeping the immaculate ledgers in the counting house of a Liverpool merchant.

If Brierley were making an income from his talents as an artist, it is hard to believe he had received any formal artistic training, rather that he was a self-taught exponent of ink-and-wash drawing. Brierley drew in Indian ink with both pen and brush. Subsequently, he applied a range of washes, mostly in greys of varying intensity, though occasionally a bright blue is introduced. Though there may be other deficiencies in Brierley's work one can appreciate the powers of observation and the skill in handling fine pen and washes that diminish almost to show the colour of the underlying paper.

He can display great powers of observation and delicacy in handling fine detail. Brierley could occasionally work well with colour is demonstrated by a fully tinted version of his depiction of the Theatre Royal, also held in the Athenaeum collection and is the cover to this publication. In many of his drawings Brierley struggles with perspective. In order to reduce these problems whenever he can he adopts a central view point in full face of his subject. The representation of inclined ground and an attempt to render bow windows are two subjects which give particular problems. The overall effect in Brierley's work is rather dark and often lowering with heavy clouds and plumes of smoke from the many chimneys of the buildings.

Another technical problem, which he seemed unable to solve, arose when he needed to depict people in his paintings. Although he can, and does, draw people in Regency dress engaged in a variety of activities – promenading, a labourer carrying a sack, a pack horse and its driver, pedestrians and market people – he usually fails to draw them in scale to their surroundings. The paintings of St John's Church and the theatre contain especially notable examples of this failure. In all the pictures where figures are included, one figure, a rather stout gentleman with a broad-brimmed hat, usually carrying a loosely furled umbrella, recurs and gives rise to speculation that here Brierley is depicting himself.

Brierley used heavy cartridge paper, and the worked surface is mainly of about 15 inches [35.5 cm] by 10 inches [25 cm], with some variation. He also produced some drawings of smaller size. All the pictures have at some time, possibly very soon after their purchase, been mounted in Bristol Board. Today the mounted drawings are stored in specially made boxes in grey, acid-free card, with maroon leather spine and corners, each labelled in gilt.

Landscape and topographical representation has been seen as the essential English art form and by the nineteenth century and the surge of the Romantic Movement, had become the form of painting which found the readiest market, a market that was enhanced by the developments in reproductive techniques which allowed printed pictures to be supplied to people of all classes. Landscape watercolours were in particular demand for use in book illustrations.

Landscape painting had its origins in the background of paintings of the Renaissance period when it was frequently used to provide a prospect against which the main subject of the painting was depicted. This technique is to be seen frequently in nativity scenes, where it sets the stable in a European landscape, often populated by contemporary figures. This approach is characteristic of the painters of northern Europe – those of Italy and the south tended to use a more idealised 'classical' setting for their paintings. In Flanders and other parts of the Netherlands, the later part of the sixteenth and, particularly, the seventeenth century saw the evolution of domestic and genre paintings. Within this tradition, landscape views were a popular form of painting; perhaps the Vermeer view of Delft is one of the best-known examples.

The depiction of landscape particularly appealed to the English market. During the eighteenth century, there emerged the English School, which is particularly associated with East Anglia and Norwich. In England there was a strong sense of attachment to the land and scenery of the areas from which persons originated. In the seventeenth century it was common to speak of 'my country' when what was implied was not Great Britain or even England but the home area of an individual. The English pastoral tradition and attachment to the countryside, especially the obsession with country estates, is manifest in painting. For example, Gainsborough's portrait of Robert and Mrs Andrews places almost as much emphasis on the landscape of their parkland as on the two subjects. It was not only in painting that this obsession can be seen but also in the vogue for landscape gardening in which Lancelot or 'Capability' Brown and Humphrey Repton constructed idealised landscapes intended to conform to certain standards of taste and fashion. It was this emphasis on the beauties of nature and on the antiquities of the past, on the romantic ruin and the 'quaint' cottage, which caused the techniques of landscape painting to be widely adopted as a way of recording a beloved view or an ancient architectural relic. The mind-set is still identifiable in the ubiquitous ideal of the urban dweller for retirement to the country, to the idealised cottage and the supposed tranquillity of rural life. This attitude is summed up in the aphorism of Cowper that 'God made the country and man-made the town'.

Watercolour is a very ancient medium, used in the illumination of manuscripts, but its widespread use by artists originated in the sixteenth century. Though used in the intervening years, especially by the limners or miniature painters, it was not until the Georgian period that the paints were widely available. It was a medium used by artists, surveyors, tourists on the Grand Tour, and on expeditions to foreign countries. Watercolour was especially popular for topographical depiction when its qualities of ease of handling, wide accessibility and quick drying times made it a useful medium. For example, one of the first 'war artists' working in the field was Paul Sandby who accompanied the army into the Highlands of Scotland immediately after the Rising of 1745. The wide availability of books giving instruction and systems of working – for example, the popular work of Alexander Cozens and others – as well as the publication of views from far flung places, ranging from the cities of southern Europe to the islands of the Pacific, created a vogue amongst amateur and professional painters for this type of work and watercolour painting of landscape became a popular recreation. Indeed, the technique and topographical subjects began to be regarded as the English 'National Art' and most of the significant painters of the period worked in the medium. Perhaps the most successful, at least in monetary terms, was Joseph Turner, who, with his new transparent technique, could produce pictures almost on a factory system. The interest in sketching and watercolour as a social accomplishment created employment for drawing masters like Brierley.

Any artist undertaking this type of work at this period invites comparison with his contemporaries working in the same field. In the case of Brierley the obvious comparison is with the work of William Gawain Herdman [1805–82]. These two artists are different in almost every respect except for their determination 'to place on record and preserve for posterity all they could collect that was valuable of the ancient appearance of their native town' [Herdman's Liverpool, W. C. M. Jackson]. Herdman came from a more prosperous family background, the son of a corn merchant who from childhood had sketched and studied the buildings and streets of Liverpool. He trained in the Liverpool Academy, an organisation from which he was subsequently expelled for his violent disagreement with the choice of Millais' 'Blind Girl' for the Academy prize. Herdman's academic training is perhaps best displayed in his essay on linear perspective published in The Art Journal 1849–50, unfortunately too late for Brierley to benefit from his ideas. Herdman exhibited landscapes in oils at the Royal Academy but mainly devoted himself to the topographical recording of Liverpool. As well as paintings of the city at the time he also specialised in historical research and reconstruction of historic landscapes. These found a ready market in his *Pictorial Relics of Ancient Liverpool*, published in four volumes between 1843 and 1878. These are a series of very skilful and fully finished watercolour views of Liverpool which display accuracy and technical and artistic merit, proving very popular and achieving wide sales. As a result Herdman achieved local celebrity status and some of his less talented eleven sons – he had four daughters as well – attempted to continue the project after William's death in 1882. The Athenaeum is fortunate that it also holds a substantial collection of Herdman pictures which makes direct comparison between his work and Brierley's possible. William Herdman chose to reconstruct the appearance of St George's Church and its surrounding 'Stock's Market' in 1734 when the church was first opened; Brierley depicts the newly rebuilt church of 1825. Herdman uses a soft watercolour technique which gives an almost blurred and dreamy feel to his painting; he also sets out to show an animated scene surrounding the church with market traders and customers and an air of bustle and business. The Brierley drawing is much more an architectural study with its hard lines and clear-cut approach. He too, in one view, shows figures in proximity to the church, but whereas Herdman's figures are in a variety of naturalistic poses, Brierley's, as so often, are stiff, posed and formalised, placed to give scale and animation to the drawing. In this aim, they fail.

A feature which establishes a connection, however tenuous, with England's premier painter, are the shop signs that appear so often in James Brierley's work. In 1762, the artist William Hogarth took an interest in the Sign Painters' Exhibition held in London. This public display made apparent the richness and diversity of the skills of the sign painters and gave Hogarth an opportunity to give his support to these craftsmen who were often regarded as mere artisans and given little credit for their abilities and talent.

The exhibition roused sufficient interest for Parliament to undertake the regulation of signs. It was ordered that they should be fastened to the wall of the building rather than suspended over the street. The majority of those shown in the Brierley images are straightforward, lettered sign boards.

However, there are others which are familiar such as the barber's pole, a conventional sign of medieval origin, and the suspended barrels with carved bunches of grapes used to mark taverns. A number of the inns have painted signs – for example, the White Bear, the Golden Lion and the Haywain are clearly shown. It is difficult to judge their artistry after they have been rendered by Brierley. The same Act of Parliament, which dealt with street signs, also authorised the numbering of houses and the placing of signs to name streets. Evidence of this practice is clearly visible in the Brierley representations. The Liverpool Corporation ordered the Act to be implemented in 1807 and the painted street names feature in many of the pictures in this collection.

If the Brierley drawings lack skill, sophistication and artistry, they have a directness of approach, a keenness of observation, a meticulous recording of detail, which makes them ideally suited for the purpose of recording for posterity what is now a vanished town which retained many features of its more primitive past. These, when Brierley worked, were rapidly disappearing to allow Liverpool to become the city of commerce of the Victorian period.

The Drawings of James Brierley

No sort of sequence or order can be gleaned from the Brierley drawings. It appears that his selection of subjects was quite arbitrary and that the drawings were done without any overriding plan. To try to make the collection more manageable, it has been divided into some sort of geographical arrangement. This is based on plotting each location on a map whereupon it becomes apparent that three divisions can be made. There is an outer ring of semi-rural points in what was then the fringe of the town but most of which would now fall in the inner-city area. The second division is an area extending from Bath Street to Russell Street and then turning west to reach the waterfront at Queen's Dock. The third division is a roughly semi-circular area which embraces the original seven streets, the developments which had taken place around them and the former area of the Pool, which in Brierley's time was the Old Dock.

Old cottages on the road to Everton from Low Hill and on Everton Brow, 1830

In his Memorials of Liverpool, J. A. Picton, writing in the 1860s, waxes lyrical about the former beauty of Everton, on its ridge with distant prospects to Cheshire and North Wales, and bemoans the loss of this landscape under the encroaching tide of streets and bricks. These two drawings by Brierley emphasise the essentially rural character of the suburb, thirty years before Picton was writing.

The rural retreat began to attract the wealthy Liverpool merchants who were seeking stylish country life within easy access of the warehouse or counting house. A pioneer of this move to Everton was George Campbell, owner of privateers, whose San Domingo House, built in 1757, commemorated a rich prize taken there. Later, ln 1803, the house was chosen as his residence by Prince William of Gloucester, who, at that time, commanded the army district of Liverpool. Soon, others followed the royal example and by the end of the century many other prominent Liverpool families had become established in Everton.

There was no church in Everton, until 1813 when the St George's Church, Everton, Act was passed and by 1814 the church was completed. Notably, this was to be the first church in the world to be constructed with an iron framework, a result of the collaboration between architect, Thomas Rickman and iron founder, John Cragg.

The Everton views chosen by Brierley are located on two of the main access roads. Everton Road ran from Low Hill (another early place of resort), past the Necropolis, to Everton Village. The cottages depicted here were located at about the midpoint of the distance between the two settlements. They present an interesting variety of styles. The two on the left are very typical of the vernacular design of the south-west Lancashire area. The central two-storeyed house has greater pretensions, though it may be that it had been enlarged and altered to make it a house of some status.

The cottages in the second picture stand on the left-hand margin of the Green in Everton Village. This was located at the point where the road from Liverpool, variously called Richmond Row and Everton Brow, intersected the road from Low Hill. Nearby was the celebrated stone-built lock-up, famous now for its appearance on the local football team's shirt crests. The Everton Toffy [sic] Shop and its neighbouring painter's establishment are of a very typical local style.

Toffee-making in Everton seems to have begun in 1759 to a recipe devised by Molly Bushel, who is said to have obtained the idea from a Liverpool doctor. Later, the sweetmeat was manufactured and sold in this cottage on Everton Brow and from a shop in London Road. The business was subsequently sold to Nobletts and the character of Mother Noblett was created as an advertising logo.

The cottage adjacent to the toffee shop was the premises of Josiah Eccles – plumber, glazier and painter. The third building was both a butcher's shop and that of Thomas Bell, a tailor. Also resident on Everton Brow was Latham Hanmer, described in the Directory as an Esquire and also as Clerk in the Collector's office at the Custom House. In these four houses is a microcosm of the early nineteenth-century social structure of Everton.

An examination of the occupations of the residents of Everton Brow and Village, as the continuation of the road was known, uncovers a scene reminiscent of Cranford. Baines' Directory lists twenty-one names. Of these, ten are listed as 'gentlewomen', though two of these, the Misses Dodson, are the proprietors of a ladies' boarding school. Two 'gentlemen' also lived in the village and one can imagine the interest that was taken in their doings by their neighbours. The more predominant was Lieutenant Colonel Nicholson, of the militia and Deputy Lord Lieutenant. Close behind in esteem must have been William Shaw who is listed as 'Constable and perpetual overseer and collector of the King's and parish taxes'. The rest of the residents come in the category of useful artisans: including two wheelwrights, two cattle dealers, a cow keeper, a shoe maker, a blacksmith, a slater, a plasterer and two cart owners. One of the local residents, who later made a fortune, was John McGeorge, a Scot, who began his career as a builder from small beginnings in Everton. He became one of the foremost of the regiment of speculative builders who erected the innumerable streets of workers' small terraced housing in Vauxhall, Everton, Anfield and Toxteth.

Cottages, left side of the road, heading from Low Hill to Everton, 1830.

Old Cottages , Everton Brow, 1830.

A view of Jackson's Tide Mill, South Shore, 1830.

James Brierley seldom chose to depict industrial buildings: this view and the drawing of the mill in Islington are the only two in the collection at the Athenaeum. The Islington mill was of a standard design, unlike that of the tide mill. Jackson's Tide Mill was located at the south end of the dock estate, in what was then a largely rural area. Lines of streets had been laid out but there was little actual building. The mill site was on the seaward side, at the junction of Northumberland Street and Sefton Street, in the district then known as Harrington, and now usually called Toxteth.

The Toxteth area was part of the estates of the Earls of Sefton and the landlords had operated a water mill, powered by a small stream which ran down the line of Northumberland Street. The site is now occupied by Brunswick Station. By 1773, the stream had largely dried up, resulting in the head of water being insufficiently strong to drive the mill and it was closed. For eighty years the site was leased from Lord Sefton by Charles Roe. Roe was the proprietor of a copper smelting works on Wapping and another on the site which became the Herculaneum Pottery. He had been anxious to diversify and, subsequently, ordered the excavation of two large reservoirs and the building of the tide mill.

In 1802, the Corporation of Liverpool made large purchases of the land in Toxteth from Lord Sefton, probably in anticipation of an eventual southern extension of the dock system, which finally came about in 1825. In October 1802, a Council resolution was approved, requiring an application to the Parliament to be made in order to purchase the land 'from the Earl of Sefton and Messrs, Roe and Leigh, which is now considered part of the township of Toxteth Park in the Parish of Walton upon the Hill … considered and taken as part of the township and parish of Liverpool'. For unexplained reasons this application was never made and it was not until the Municipal Reform Act of 1835 that parts of Toxteth were incorporated into Liverpool.

In anticipation of a southward extension of the dock estate in 1811, the Dock Committee had tried to negotiate the acquisition of the tide mill but it was not until 1827 that a jury was empanelled to assess the values of properties in the area. The tide mill was described as having two reservoirs, mill, machinery and a dwelling house. Eventually, William Jackson, the proprietor of the mill at the time, was awarded £50,000 in compensation. The construction of what was to become Brunswick Dock began in 1827, to a combined design of Rennie and Hartley.

If the date ascribed to this picture by Brierley is correct, and is not a reworking of an earlier sketch, the mill must have been on the point of closure and demolition. Jackson's Mill demonstrated the use of the daily ebb and flow of tidal water to power mills. This is a very ancient technology, with examples from the seventh century being excavated in Northern Ireland. Examples of surviving tidal mills can be seen at Woodbridge in Suffolk and at Eling in Hampshire. Today, tidal power is once more being viewed as a source of renewable energy, widely accessible and free. Its use is limited to sites which are extensive enough for the mill and its reservoirs, where there is an adequate tidal flow, and a wide tidal range. Extensive engineering is necessary to build reservoirs and channels. Creation of the mill ponds at Jackson's Mill, for example, required the excavation of ten acres of land.

Tide mills operate by storing water in an estuary or artificial pond at high tide. The mill wheel turns during the water's ingress and, at low tide, the impounded water is released through a channel, which again drives the waterwheel. The site leased by Mr Roe provided an ideal environment for tidal power.

It is apparent from the drawing that some considerable care had been taken in the design of the building. Architectural sophistication is displayed in the dentil cornice to the main building, the elaborate lintels of the windows with their false keystones, and in the large double door with a blocked architrave. What Brierley does not show are the two reservoirs, or lodges, popularly known as Jackson's Dam, that were excavated for the purpose of storing the water. The larger one, of about 8½ acres, lay behind the artist, while the smaller one of 1½ acres, which acted as a header reserve, lay on the other side of the building. The picture shows that the adjoining house was of some luxury, reflecting the importance and prosperity of the miller.

In 1821, the mill was being operated by Francis Lee Jones, described in Gore's Directory as a flour dealer and baker in Tabley Street. In Baines' Directory of 1825, Jones is shown to have expanded his activities to include dealing in groceries. By 1829, William Jackson had become the miller. He is probably the same William Jackson who is listed, together with his partner, Henderson, in 1824 as millwrights, iron founders and French-burrstone makers. French burrstones were the best quality mill stones and, perhaps, it is an example of their work that is propped

against the mill wall. In Brierley's study there are several squared stone blocks lying on the ground between the mill and the shore line. It may be that these are blocks of stone waiting for conversion into mill stones or that they are material for the dock works that were taking place. In the background of the picture, we catch a glimpse of the river, on which two vessels are shown. One is a small, single-masted, gaff-rigged sloop. Though only very sketchily drawn, this is probably intended to be a Mersey Flat – the sailing barge which plied in the estuary and coastal waters. The other ship is a schooner-rigged paddle steamer, one of the steam packets which plied between Liverpool and the upper Mersey estuary. In 1829, services to Runcorn and Weston Point, Ellesmere Port, the Chester Canal, Ince (on the alarmingly named Vesuvius) and Eastham are all advertised.

A view of the old public house, London Road, opposite the King's Monument, 1828

This inn was built in the seventeenth century, on the edge of the Great Heath, an area which provided rough grazing and supplies of stone, clay and fuel for the Burgesses of Liverpool. The heath extended from this point to the boundary of Everton.

By 1726 a turnpike road had opened, its first gate being adjacent to the tavern at the point where London Road and Pembroke Place diverged.

The elevation of the ridge and its openness to sea breezes made it an ideal site to build windmills; during the early eighteenth century three were constructed in the area. A water mill was added later, which is depicted on Eyes' map of 1785, and was used for seed crushing. The tavern in Brierley's drawing took a new name from the windmill that was built on the junction of Stafford Street and London Road. This mill, which acquired the grisly name of Gallows Mill, was built in 1715 and remained in situ until 1788 when it was bought by the Corporation who were anxious to develop the area as a fashionable suburb. Today [2017], the site is occupied by a large department store.

The space before the mill was the site of part of Folly Fair, a festival that was held annually in the vicinity. The fair had its early origins in the Easter celebrations and was centred on a belvedere tower of eight storeys, surrounded by gardens, built in Islington by Mr Gibson, the proprietor of the Theatre Royal. After the demolition in 1780 of the tower and pleasure grounds – known as Gibson's Folly – a new home was sought for the fair. It continued in the space in front of the Mill Inn and the junction of the two roads. The fair was eventually closed down in the nineteenth century, having become infamous for disorderly conduct and drunkenness.

The soubriquet 'The Gallows Inn' recalled a grim episode in 1716. In the previous year, an invasion to assert the right of James Edward, son of James II, to the throne in place of the German King George I, had been launched from Scotland. At Preston, on 12 November 1715, the rebel army was surrounded and forced to surrender: 1,485 prisoners were taken.

The loyalty of much of Lancashire to the Hanoverian regime was suspect but Liverpool had been staunch in its rejection of the Jacobite claims. Consequently, the rank and file captives taken at Preston were to be tried at a special assize in Liverpool. The judges arrived on 11 January 1716, undoubtedly with instructions to make examples of some of the rebels. Of those tried in Liverpool between 20 January and 9 February, sixty-seven were found guilty and seven acquitted. The trials stopped when the remaining prisoners, pleading guilty, were sentenced to transportation to the West Indies as white indentured servants – a profitable cargo for some Liverpool merchants.

Four prisoners, George Collingwood, Archibald Burnett, Alexander Drummond and John Hunter, were sentenced to death by hanging at Liverpool. The executions took place on 25 February on a scaffold erected on the junction of London Road and Pembroke Place.

Almost the same spot was chosen in 1816 for the statue of King George III. This had been proposed in 1809 to commemorate the monarch's fifty-year reign and was originally intended to stand, appropriately, in Great George Square. A ceremonial foundation stone was placed there but, despite a grant from the Corporation, the public subscription was not taken up with enthusiasm.

A further grant from the Corporation allowed the commissioning of Richard Westmacott to provide the sculpture. Westmacott based the design of the pose and costume on the memorial to Marcus Aurelius in Rome, only modelling the King's face on life. His features were described by one historian as 'by no means indicative of great intellectual powers'. The project was eventually completed in March 1821, when it was decided by the organising committee that a better location for the statue might be 'in the centre of the wide part of London Road'.

Brierley's picture emphasises the changing character of the London Road area. The inn is typical of the period of perhaps 150 years earlier, with its low profile, its small windows and its low-pitched, stone-flagged roof, contrasting with the contemporary residential terraces about it. The inn looks exactly what it was – a rural relic caught up in the urban sprawl of the expanding town.

A view of the old cottage (sign of the Ship) between Mount Pleasant & Brownlow Hill, 1828

This inn is clearly identifiable on Baines' map of 1821 as the solitary building on that part of Mount Pleasant, which at this point follows the workhouse wall to join Brownlow Hill. Originally, this diversion was to avoid the Moss Lake Fields, a swampy, marshy area, much valued for its turbary, that is, the right to dig peat as fuel. On the right-hand side of the road, at the junction where the Medical Institution (1836) stands today was the inn and bowling green, which in 1752 was kept by William Roscoe and where his son, also William, was born. Today [2017] the site of the Ship Inn is the car park which lies between the Student Guild building of the University of Liverpool and the Lifelong Learning Centre (formerly the School of Hygiene). Immediately opposite is the Metropolitan Cathedral, which stands on the site of the workhouse.

The Ship Inn shown here is of considerable antiquity. The design of the building conforms, as far as can be judged, to the plan of farmhouses of the seventeenth century (see Pembroke Road Cottage page 47). It is difficult to assess whether the Ship Inn was built as an ale house or was a conversion with an additional door inserted. The stone for the walls of both the building and the boundary wall of the adjacent land, together with stone roofing slates, was doubtless taken from the large stone delph, or quarry, at the intersection of Brownlow Hill and Mount Pleasant.

By the early nineteenth century, the area was being developed. The so-called 'Rector's Fields', which funded the Warbrick Charity, had been sold for building, and Baines' map shows the proposed layout of the streets as a neat, rectangular grid. The Ship Inn was a building which would soon disappear as development of the district took place. Most of the housing erected on these new streets has been swallowed up by the university but enough remains to give an impression of the solid Georgian terraces that once filled them.

The area at the summit of Mount Pleasant, formerly Martindale Hill, became the site to which a number of Liverpool's charitable and public institutions had been moved. At the top of Brownlow Street, the new Infirmary had replaced the old hospital on Shaw's Brow in 1824. Built to the design of John Foster, at a cost of £27,800, in the classical Doric style, it was thought, at the time, to be a forbidding building.

The work of the Vestry in administering the Poor Law has already been mentioned. This responsibility put them in charge of what was reputed to be the largest workhouse in the country, sometimes with as many as 6,000 residents. When the old workhouse in Hanover Street became too small and dilapidated for the numbers involved, a decision was taken to build new premises on Brownlow Hill. The work was authorised on 26 August 1769 and steps were taken to buy in stocks of building materials at an advantageous price. The completed building was four storeys high, built in brick, with stone facings and constructed around a quadrangle. A turret with a clock was placed in the centre of the main façade.

In 1776, an adjacent House of Correction was erected to provide a short but salutary taste of imprisonment and penal servitude for minor delinquents. In 1806, to exploit the relative isolation of the area, a totally separate House of Recovery – a facility intended as an isolation unit for the victims of fevers – was built in the grounds of the workhouse.

The several almshouses which had been endowed in Liverpool, with the exception of the Molyneux Charity houses in Hanover Street, had been located near the old infirmary and the Haymarket since 1748. In 1787, it was agreed to build new premises on Martindale Hill and to remove all the almshouses to that place.

Thus most of the social and charitable concerns of the Parish, and later the Parish Offices, were concentrated on Mount Pleasant, well away from the most heavily developed residential areas. At the time it was argued that this elevated location with its abundance of fresh winds was healthy and, when the best medical opinion favoured the atmospheric theory of the spread of disease it had an obvious logic. The fresh air would disperse the threat of infection and the direction of the prevailing winds would ensure that any poisonous miasmas would be dissipated over the surrounding countryside. In these more cynical days, we might wonder if at least part of the intention was to keep the 'objects of charity', the paupers and the unsavoury malefactors away from the sight of respectable citizens.

Doubtless, the presence of these institutions was regarded by William Hastie, landlord of the Ship Inn, as a bonus. Visiting tradesmen, administrators, clergy, lawyers, family, and friends would need refreshment after their exhausting walk up the hill and he was uniquely placed to meet this need.

A view of ten cottages between New Bird Street and Greenland Street, 1830

The dwellings depicted in this picture are very different from the majority of Brierley's views. The immediate impression is of industrial housing in a Lancashire mill town. It is obvious that they are of no great age and do not have any of the picturesque qualities of most of Brierley's other subjects. The cottages stood on the east side of Flint Street, which ran northwards from Parliament Street, parallel with the river, and was intersected by Greenland Street and New Bird Street. The terrace comprised ten houses, each of three floors with a single room on each storey. The manuscript copy of the census return for 1801 confirms that these were so-called 'front

houses' (i.e. not built back to back, as discussed earlier). The census return of 1801 lists 12 names as residents of Flint Street but little other information is forthcoming. These were not the sort of people listed in directories, an impression confirmed by the information for New Bird Street given in the census return. Seventeen occupations of householders are specifically listed, and the rest are categorised as general workers. The lists confirm that the area was closely associated with the sea: ten are 'Mariners' – one of whom is listed as 'At sea'; three are Excise Officers and four are labourers.

It seems possible that the cottages were built to house workers and mariners engaged in the whalefishing trade, as the oil house where blubber was rendered to oil was adjacent, at the foot of Parliament Street. Liverpool's engagement in the Greenland Whale Fishery (hence Greenland Street) began in 1750 and by the end of the century, was a major occupation. The quarry was the Greenland right whale, which provided oil for lamps, medicinal purposes, lubricating oil and whale bone for ladies' clothing. In 1824 there were 32 stay-makers in Liverpool. Whaling reached its peak in 1778 but by 1826 only one whaler was left, the Baffin, designed and captained by the most distinguished of Liverpool whaling masters, William Scorseby. The son of a celebrated Whitby whaler and navigator, Scoresby came to Liverpool in 1819. He was not only a consummate seaman but had studied science and navigation at Edinburgh University and became a Fellow of the Royal Society of that city. His subsequent whaling voyages took on the colour of a scientific investigation, surveying the coast and recording meteorological conditions. After the death of his wife in 1822, the declining trade and his deep religious convictions drew him into training for the ministry of the Church of England. From 1826, Scoresby was the curate of the Floating Church in George's Dock.

William Scorseby 1789–1857
William Scoresby's youth was spent partly in accompanying his father's pioneering arctic whaling voyages and partly in study at Edinburgh University. At the age of 21 he commanded a ship and was able to make very useful observations in meteorology and magnetism. In 1818, he moved to Liverpool and soon after, on the death of his wife, entered the ministry of the Church of England. Scoresby served as Chaplain to the Floating Chapel and other churches while continuing scientific research, especially into magnetism. [Athenaeum Proprietor No. 19]

A vivid picture of the methods and conditions of the Greenland Fishery is provided by the painting attributed to the so-called 'Ribbon Artist' (c.1800–1820) of the barque James, in the collection of the Maritime Museum of the National Museums and Galleries, Liverpool. The former French twenty-gun privateer had been re-rigged and is shown amidst the ice, with her whale boats in the water with their harpooners ready to strike, in pursuit of two whales. In the background can be seen other ships of the fleet – unlike the sperm whale fishery of the Pacific, northern ships often worked in a flotilla. The picture also shows a party which has landed on an ice floe to kill seals for their skins and meat. When the whales were killed, the blubber and bone were removed and the former was packed in casks and brought back to Liverpool to be 'Tried Out' – that is, rendered down.

A. Mosses del.

E. Smith sculp.

A view of the old coffee house, North Shore, occupied by Mr Vandries, 1805

The Van Dries, a family of Dutch origin, left a permanent memorial to their business in the name Vandries Street, which runs between Great Howard Street and Waterloo Road. Today, Vandries Street is lined with warehouses and semi-derelict buildings. In the early nineteenth century, however, when the wide sandy shore stretched from New Quay to as far as the new resort of Southport and the Ribble estuary, the beach at the end of the lane in question was a popular family retreat. The sands were lined with dunes and only interrupted by the peaty remains of the submerged post-glacial forest, now largely eroded or built over.

The central block of the coffee house would appear to date from the early to mid-seventeenth century, with its stone mullioned windows, square drip-mouldings and attic dormer windows so typical of houses of the period. Several extensions have been made, probably to accommodate visitors in search of refreshment. The left-hand block is decorated with a carving of a female figure, quite possibly the figurehead of a vessel. In the background can be seen the wind-powered oil-seed crushing mill of Earles and Carter. To add to the amenities of the area, a white lead works was located at the junction of Charters Street and Waterloo Road. The maps drawn by Horwood in 1803 show that there was a bowling green behind the main block of Vandries Coffee House and, a little further inland, what appear to be formal pleasure grounds. For good measure, Brierley animates the scene by including several figures, one of which is again the stout gentleman with the umbrella.

The North Shore was devoted to sea bathing, where the Van Dries family operated a fleet of bathing machines. These were cabins on wheels from which anxious bathers were attended in the water by stalwart dippers, locally known as 'Dowkers'. Minding the clothes of those who chose to bathe but not to avail themselves of a machine was a source of income for a tribe of urchins who lurked around the dunes. On the North Shore, a publican named Sommerton maintained two large static caravans for the less delicate of disposition, providing changing rooms for forty or fifty people at a time, which were well patronised. However, many of the men, and not a few of the ladies, bathed without these refinements and became so much a common sight that their nudity was no longer remarked upon. Even the delicate Ellen Weeton could say '… the latter is not the most pleasant sight; but I am now accustomed to it, that really I do not feel so much shocked as I ought to do' (Miss Weeton's Journal of a Governess, ed. Bagley, Newton Abbot, 1969, p.181).

The bathing machines are included in a view of the North Shore amongst W. G. Herdman's pictures of Liverpool. In the Herdman painting, the Van Dries house is shown on the right-hand side, while the foreground is crowded with bathing machines, from one of which a bather emerges. In Herdman's rendering of the scene, holiday-makers walk the sands and paddle on the edge of the sea. A stall sells food and customers sit at tables, while a vendor with a covered tray wanders between them.

Though today we find it difficult to envisage the Kirkdale shore as a holiday place reputed for its sea bathing, we have to remember that, at the time, the north bank of the Mersey estuary was lined with other watering places. In his 1795 Guide Book, Dr Moss recommends Bootle as a place '…where genteel company resort for the sea bathing and sea air in the summer season. Here are public ordinaries, [eating places or restaurants] lodgings and other permanent accommodations.' A few miles further north, the new development at Crosby Sea Bank or Waterloo provided a similar facility, with its shore-side terraces of 'cottages'.

A view of the cottage in The Field, north side of Pembroke Road 1830

At least one previous commentator on this picture has asserted that, as there was no Pembroke Road in Liverpool, the description must be incorrect and that, consequently, this view must be of houses in Pembroke Place. This is not so: Baines' 'Map of Liverpool' of 1825 shows quite clearly that the street which continued the line of Pembroke Place beyond the junction with Crown Street and Boundary Place was Pembroke Road. The cluster of houses can be picked out on the map quite easily, as the north side of the road had no buildings except for this group of three, set back from the main street at the end of a short lane or drive.

Pembroke Road provided a link between the newly built residential street of Pembroke Place and the rural retreats of Mount Vernon and Edge Hill. This idea of the buildings shown being a rural arcadia is reinforced by the use of the name 'The Cottage', which reflects the fashionable fancy for the pastoral life that prevailed in the last decades of the eighteenth century. Of course, the house shown here is no more a cottage than Marie Antoinette's dairy farm at Versailles was a genuine agricultural enterprise.

The main house, shown facing the viewer, is a substantial building of two floors, with an outshut or lean-to annexe extension behind the main block. The chimney of this and a raised portion of the roof can be seen behind the central chimney stack. The fact that the building has this penthouse and that the front entrance is off-set from the centre point could be taken to suggest that it is a rebuilt – or at least re-fronted – farmhouse of mid-seventeenth century date. A typical design for this type of house was an arrangement of three rooms with the front entrance one-third of the way along the frontage. Inside, to the right of the entrance passageway, would lie the dairy and store rooms; to the left a large living room, known as the hall or kitchen, and beyond that a parlour for the family.

It may be observed that the house in the background has the modern accessory of a lightning rod. The invention of the lightning conductor has been ascribed to Benjamin Franklin in about 1752 and, in the later years of the century, there was great controversy between British scientists who insisted that the rod must be tipped by a ball and the Americans who thought all that was necessary was a simple point. Here the design was sturdily British.

It is not possible to deduce the occupants of these three houses from the directories. Baines lists ten residents of Pembroke Road in 1825 and we can see a similarity with the dwellers in Everton Village; though the artisan element is missing, we have a colony of 'Gentlefolk' comprised of Margaret Dean, Edward Jee and John Wulf. In the language of the period, this implies that they were living on investment income. Their neighbours were of the mercantile class – a tobacco manufacturer, two corn merchants, and a cotton broker. A mariner, Thomas Brassey, lived here, though by 1829 he was listed as a merchant. Captain Hamilton also lived in the road but the directories give no clue as to whether he was a soldier or a naval man.

A number of residential suburban villages existed around Liverpool as they did near many other towns. However, the pattern on Merseyside was unusual in that there was comparable development across the Mersey, in Cheshire and the Wirral. The longstanding existence of the various Mersey ferries allowed this development to take place long before improved land transport links facilitated the growth of suburbs in the more distant villages around the town.

A view of the house, top of Duke Street, opposite Rodney Street, 1830

This particular picture of Brierley's leaves less scope for comment than most of the others. The house, occupied by James Gardener, a wine and spirit merchant, is largely concealed; the perimeter wall obscures most of the details and only the upper floor is visible. However, there is a particular interest this house and its surroundings, not least because it must have been the last of the buildings portrayed by Brierley to be demolished. It was intact until the 1980s when it was acquired by John Moores University and a new building of sympathetic design rose on its site.

The area at the top of Duke Street – a tree-lined avenue in 1769 – remained largely rural, except for sporadic quarrying activity, until c.1780 when urban encroachment began. It was a highly desirable area on the fringe of the existing town, with the advantage of a hill-top view and air clear of the pall of smoke which must have hung over Liverpool, if Brierley's depiction of smoking chimneys on every building is to be believed.

Rodney Street, its name commemorating Admiral Lord Rodney, victor in the Battle of the Saintes, 1780, had been projected and begun, principally by William Roscoe in 1783–4. It was built up in a piecemeal fashion over the next two decades by speculative builder/developers such as Daniel Stackhouse, himself responsible for a terrace of six houses at the Duke Street end of the street.

The house in the painting is not shown on the Eyes plan of 1765 – although that corner of the map is obscured by the vignette of the Town Hall – but the impression given is that the whole area comprised fields under cultivation. When Charles Eyes prepared his survey of 1785, the house was built and is clearly marked. Similarly, Horwood's map of 1803 depicts a building whose plan coincides with an interpretation of Brierley's drawing. It shows a house built on a U-shaped plan with two wings and a central block. The wing on the west side was devoted to stables and services. The house is enclosed by a substantial wall and there are extensive gardens and pleasure grounds laid out within the perimeter.

The top of the hill at this point had, for many years, been a substantial quarry of yellow sandstone which had been used extensively in the building of the town. St Thomas' Church, St Paul's Church, St John's Church and the Town Hall façade had all been built with stone extracted from what was often known as Quarry Hill. Horwood's map shows how the quarry had extended from the summit of the ridge down the slope to the line of Rathbone Street. This part of the quarry was separated from the main delph by a ridge of spoil heaps.

The margin of the quarries provided a popular promenade for the people of the town who could enjoy the fresh air and extensive views. During the severe winter of 1767, a work creation scheme led to the landscaping of the promenade. This parade could be approached through a tunnel which connected the quarries to Upper Duke Street and which had been used for the transportation of stone. Originally known as Mount Zion, that name fell from favour after the opening of a public house was deemed to make the use of such a name blasphemous. After 1774, when St James' Church was built, the name St James' Mount became generally used for the walk. The discovery of a spring in the eastern wall of the quarry, at a time when hydrotherapy was fashionable, led Doctor Houlston to claim the water was especially efficacious for the treatment of eye complaints and, for many years, it was a place frequented by the townspeople and visitors. A stone tablet marks the site of the spring today.

A portion of the reclaimed land was leased out for building and it may very well be that the house we are examining was built at this time. In 1825 the town faced a problem of insufficient space for cemeteries. The situation of the Non-conformist chapels, which usually lacked a burial ground, was even worse and in 1823 a number of prominent dissenters formed a company and purchased land in Everton Road, on the eastern fringe of the town, for a 'Necropolis'.

In 1825, inspired by this development and concerned by the declining respectability of St James' Mount, the Rector, the Reverend Jonathan Brooks, suggested the purchase of the derelict quarry and its transformation into a cemetery for members of the established church. The Corporation accepted the suggestion and the site was purchased. Landscaping work began under the direction of John Foster Junior who contributed the design for the mortuary chapel, now known as the Oratory, where services prior to interment were held. This Oratory is one of the very few of Foster's buildings which has survived intact. It has a Doric portico and is a perfect reconstruction of a small Greek temple. One of the first important funerals that took place in the St James' Cemetery was that of William Huskisson, killed at the opening of the Liverpool and Manchester Railway in September 1830. The mausoleum which surmounts his grave is another work by Foster, with a statue carved by John Gibson.

A view of St Anne's Church, 1830

The church of St Anne, on the northern fringe of the town, was founded in 1770 by Mr Thomas Dobb, a wealthy cabinet maker with premises in Williamson Square. Building work was completed two years later. At that time, the site of the church lay in countryside and it was some years before the surrounding streets were developed; St Anne Street is outlined, but without any building development on a map of 1785, and it was over the next ten years that it grew as the fashionable housing area that we see in this drawing. St Anne's was the church chosen by William Roscoe for his wedding to Jane Griffies on 22 February, 1781. The first vicar of the church was Claudius Crigan who became Bishop of Sodor and Man in 1784. His patron in this episcopal appointment was the Duchess of Athol who expected that Crigan's frail health would shortly allow the succession of her young son, then a minor. Crigan disappointed her hopes and lived another 25 years, outliving his intended successor. Crigan's tenure at St Anne's was marked by a celebrated case in the Court of King's Bench when the twin rectors of Liverpool used the loose wording of the Act establishing St Anne's to challenge the right of Crigan to celebrate marriages in the church.

There is no record of the name of the architect, but the plain brick exterior shows no particular talent in its designer. Some attempt was made to give it a fashionable appearance in the Gothic style by

the installation of ogee windows and the rather useless and feeble pinnacles on the tower and parapet. St Anne's was unusual in its positioning, as the main axis of the church was on a north–south line rather than the more usual east–west orientation. At a later date, an effort to improve the appearance of the building was made, and the brickwork was covered with stucco. J. A. Picton opined that this 'brought out with better effect its incarnate ugliness' [Memorials of Liverpool, J. A. Picton, Longmans 1875].

For many years the church was the main venue for the concerts of the Liverpool Choral Society and its annual music festival. On these occasions, artistes, both amateur and professional, performed a variety of works, including some of the earliest performances in the town of Handel's oratorios.

An insight into the way this area developed as a fashionable suburb can be gained from the fact, that for some years, it had many distinguished residents. The Judges' Lodgings were adjacent to the church; Matthew Gregson, the patron of artists and an eminent historian and author lived nearby; and one house was used as the officers' mess of regiments stationed in Liverpool.

Many of the other houses were occupied by wealthy business men, lawyers and doctors, including the celebrated Dr Rutter, founder of both the Athenaeum and the Liverpool Medical Institution and Library. In 1846, the Judges' Lodgings were thought worthy enough to provide hospitality for the Prince Consort when he attended the opening of the Albert Dock.

The original church stood in the path of the extension of St Anne Street in a northward direction, planned in 1867. As a result the church shown in this view was demolished and a new building by Robson, the Corporation architect, was built on a plot to the east of its old site. Today this once fashionable area is covered with industrial premises and dual carriageway roads and shows no evidence of its distinguished past.

Matthew Gregson 1748/9–1824
Gregson was one of the group in Liverpool, which included William Roscoe, who devoted themselves to the development of art and culture in the town. He was keenly interested in antiquarian studies and history. His book Fragments, which contains notes and illustrations of the antiquities of Lancashire, is still an invaluable source for the history of the county. [Athenaeum Proprietor No. 99]

Two views of St Luke's Church, 1830

Of all the major buildings depicted in the drawings of James Brierley, St Luke's is the only one which is still in existence, even if only as the ruins of the tower and outer walls. Severely damaged in the Second World War, its elegant remains have become accepted as a memorial to the 4,000 victims of the Liverpool Blitz. Though it does not have official status, on two occasions, plans for its demolition have been nullified by popular opinion. Today, the grounds contain a monument to the victims of the Irish Famine and, it seems, the church's status as a memorial is assured. The church with its elegant tower stands at an important road junction, is clearly seen from many angles and neatly closes the views up Renshaw Street and Bold Street.

Like the other places of worship, St Luke's was a response to the rapidly expanding residential areas of Liverpool and their growing populations. The site, acquired in 1791, was known as the 'Pump Fields' as it was where the water pipes of the Corporation were made and stored. The first record of any proposal to build can be found in the Corporation records for 3 June 1801 when the Council received a letter from Mr Bardswell, on behalf of the residents of Bold Street, requesting that a church should be built and the living given to a Mr Sanderson.

On 6 February 1802, the scheme advanced when the design by John Foster the Elder was accepted, with the specification that there was adequate seating for the poor. Before the work could start, the approval of the Rectors of the Parish of Liverpool had to be sought. All churches and chapels within the town that had been built were considered to be chapels of the parish churches. Consequently, the two Rectors were entitled to a proportion of the tithes and dues of the new churches, whose priests had the ecclesiastical status of chaplains or curates. This consent of the Rectors was given and the Reverend John Sanderson was accepted as the incumbent. Thus, with all the conditions in place, the final agreement to the construction of the new church was given and Foster's plans approved. For reasons now unknown, the work did not begin until 1810 when, on 10 February, the Finance Committee of the Corporation was directed to make the necessary funds available. By 1819 some building work had been done but a block was put on further expenditure and progress was delayed for two years. It is a suggestion that, like so many of Foster's projects, it was exceeding the budget and when work resumed in 1821 it was under the supervision of his son, John Foster the younger. At this point, the plans were changed and a new approach to ecclesiastical design was adopted. Many churches of this period were designed as rectangular auditoria with a small recess to contain the altar.

John Foster 1787–1846
The second son of John Foster, the architect of the Exchange and the Athenaeum, the younger Foster received his early training in the office of Jeffry Wyatt (later Wyattville) and from 1809 spent several years abroad. He travelled in Greece and Italy in the company of C. R. Cockerell. His studies in the classical world determined much of his later work in Liverpool. His best known buildings were the Custom House and the mortuary chapel at St James' Cemetery. Today only a very small amount of his work survives. He created a

preference for the classical style for public buildings in Liverpool though, as exemplified in St Luke's Church, he could work successfully in the Gothic style. [Athenaeum Proprietor No. 295/246]

North East View, of St Luke's Church, Liverpool.

Foster the younger adopted the Gothic tradition and designed a nave in a Perpendicular style with a tower, its lower stages of a Perpendicular design, surmounted by an upper storey of 'Decorated' style with panel work and ogee arches – an historically impossible sequence. When building recommenced in 1821, a decision had been made to add a chancel – a very early manifestation of the influence of the ecclesiologists. It is possible that the chancel, which adopts a rather florid Perpendicular style with buttresses and pinnacles, was the work of either the younger Foster, perhaps with some input from Rickman, or from an assistant, Edwards, in Foster's office. Certainly, we know that Foster the younger asked permission to make both internal and external alterations. One of the cleverest touches in the

design of St Luke's is the way in which the west front stands on an impressive flight of steps. This raises it above its surroundings and adds to the striking impression of the distant view. The building was eventually completed in 1831, at the enormous cost of £53,418.

Presumably as a result of the delays, the Reverend John Sanderson was never heard of again and the first incumbent of the new church was a Liverpool man, the Reverend James Aspinall, whose father had been Mayor of Liverpool in 1803. Aspinall proved a popular choice and established a reputation as a writer and speaker. He was the author of Liverpool a Few Years Since, using the nom de plume of 'An Old Stager', a book that is now a useful source of information on the town's society at that time.

In its early years, St Luke's was surrounded by a stone wall but this was demolished, the stones sold and the whole replaced by the cast-iron railing of these pictures. In true Foster tradition, the work was kept in the family: these palings were cast by Foster and Griffin, of which John's younger brother, James, was the principal partner. Family influence did not end there: John Foster was not only the architect but also the building contractor. Another Foster brother, William, was the contractor for the glass and its installation. The contract for the masonry was awarded to the firm of Hetherington and Grindrod, which was also connected to the Foster family. Given the family's record it may be a simple coincidence that St Luke's was finished late and hugely over budget.

A North West View, of St Luke's Church, Liverpool, 1830.

Brierley's picture of the north-west view is taken from a viewpoint on the junction of Renshaw and Bold Streets. Leece Street runs away from the viewer on the left, while Berry Street diverges to the right. The entrance to Bold Place can be seen immediately beyond the church railings, while in the distance is the tower of St Mark's in Duke Street.

The north-east view was made looking down Leece Street and shows the very spot, at the head of Bold Street, from which the previous picture was made. It is apparent that Bold Street was already well provided with shops. The needle-like spire on the left of the picture is that of St Michael's in Upper Pitt Street

Brierley enlivens his views with passers-by and the familiar shape of the stout gentleman with his umbrella appears in both of them.

A View of St Mark's Church, Upper Duke Street, 1830

On 6 August 1800, the Reverend Thomas Jones and a group of associates, led by James Brooke, petitioned the Corporation for permission to build a church in Duke Street. Once permission had finally been granted, the church, dedicated to St Mark, was built, in brick, close to the junction with Berry Street, at a cost of £18,000. The design lacked any inspiration – the sole ornament was the feeble tower with its corner urns and even this was demolished as unsafe in 1830.

The original subscribers to the application began to be concerned about the future of their foundation. On 6 October 1802, James Brandreth, a member of an important medical family, on behalf of the proprietors, approached the Corporation to ask them to assume the patronage and responsibility for the church. After consideration, however, the request was turned down. The Corporation was planning the building of St Luke's Church close by and did not want the liability for two churches so close together. The Bishop of Chester, Henry Majenie (1800–09), seems to have been reluctant to issue a licence for the performance of services. Consequently, although St Mark's was opened for worship in 1803, it was not consecrated until 1815. Before the church was opened, its tale of misfortune began. The Reverend Jones died suddenly whilst on a journey to London. His place as incumbent was taken by the Reverend Richard Blacow who held the living at West Derby and who was to hold the two offices for more than forty years until his death in 1847.

On the opening of the church in 1803, the misfortunes continued. The service attracted a large crowd and people were crushed into the church. At some point, a bench was overturned, panic escalated and the ensuing stampede resulted in many serious injuries.

In 1820, Blacow and St Mark's obtained a national notoriety. Blacow, a man of extreme views, was a fervent, venomous and vehement preacher, obsessed by the reports of the behaviour of Queen Caroline. On 27 January 1821 he preached a sermon, later issued as a pamphlet, attacking her as 'Goddess of lust on the pedestal of shame [who] after exhibiting her claims to their favour [of radicals and revolutionaries] in two distinct quarters of the globe – after compassing sea and land with her guilty paramour to gratify to the full her impure desires and even polluting the Holy Sepulchre with her presence … returned to this hallowed soil so hardened in sin, so bronzed with infamy, so callous of every feeling of decency or shame.'

The Queen's Attorney General, Henry Brougham, brought an action for libel in the Court of King's Bench on 1 September 1821. The trial attracted great public attention and the courtroom was packed with an eager throng. The prosecution was led by Mr Tindal who opened with a diatribe on the infamy of a clergyman holding and expressing such views. He described Blacow as 'a meddling, intriguing turbulent priest'. Witnesses were brought forward to verify that Blacow had indeed preached the sermon and that it had subsequently been published. The evidence was sufficient and after a vicious summing-up, Blacow was sentenced to a fine of £100 and six months in the prison of the Marshalsea.

A view of St Martin's Church, 1830

The site of St Martin's lay on the former town fields previously farmed by the burgesses of Liverpool. In the eighteenth century, many of the owners gave up their agricultural activities and sold their land for housing. The development of the district as a residential area necessitated the provision of a church to serve the community. Funding for such church building was available from the Commissioners of the Treasury who, by an Act of 1818, had been allotted £1,000,000 for the provision of churches in new urban areas. Often known as 'Waterloo Churches', the 300 churches funded by the Commissioners between 1819 and 1830 were seen as a national offering of thanks for the defeat of the French. Additionally, the Church of England, alarmed by the growing strength and influence of the Non-conformist sects and Methodism in urban areas, was determined to heighten its own presence in such places.

The Commissioners outlined the general principles of the style and design of the new churches. Essentially, the plan was to provide a large auditorium with seating accommodation increased by the erection of galleries. The design was to be simple with the most economical materials used. For the sake of economy, the new industrial materials, such as brick, cast iron and stucco, were often employed for pillars, stairs and furnishings. It was understood that either the Grecian or the Gothic style could be used but any additional expenditure on decorative features was to be met from other sources, be they private subscriptions or local grants.

In 1825, Richard Houghton, a wealthy timber merchant resident in Hunter Street, gave a piece of land in what was then called Great Oxford Street (now Sylvester Street) for the provision of a church and burial ground. An initial problem was that it seemed likely that the terminus of the new Liverpool and Manchester Railway would encroach on the site, but this was solved when the decision was made in 1830 to make the terminus of the line at Crown Street.

An Act of Parliament was obtained vesting the patronage of this new church in the Corporation. On 13 November 1828, a Special Vestry met to make the decisions about the building and its parochial organisation. John Foster the younger's design proved more expensive than anticipated and additional funds had to be granted. Two clergy were appointed – Reverend J. B. Monk and Reverend Nicholas Robinson – as first and second minister, respectively. Attached to the new church was an extensive graveyard which reached down from the site to Vauxhall Road. It was a measure to counter the sanitary difficulties raised by the overcrowding of the old parish cemeteries at St Peter's and St Nicholas' which were becoming filled to capacity and a health threat to the town.

Foster's Gothic design diverges from the more severe Commissioners' churches in its possession of a considerable spire and many of the architectural trimmings of the Gothic style, some of which were made in cast iron. The Gothic style of the church was appropriate for the newly fashionable 'High Church' or Anglo-Catholic Movement, with its emphasis on the Christian sacraments, a revival of ritual and on the Apostolic Succession of the Church of England.

In this picture, Brierley makes an effort to give human interest to this view of what was a brand-new church. The fashionably-dressed couple walks rather stiffly down Oxford Street in the direction of Vauxhall Road. The junction of Lime Kiln Lane can be seen in the bottom left corner of the drawing.

St Philip's Church, Hardman Street, 1830

St Philip's Church on the corner of Hardman Street (named after John Hardman, MP for Liverpool in 1754) is one of the results of a powerful architectural collaboration between the iron master John Cragg of the Mersey Foundry and Thomas Rickman, the architect. These were the men responsible for the churches of St Michael-in-the-Hamlets and St George's, Everton, which, like St Philip's, combined the structural and decorative use of cast iron in combination with brick or stone. The church was, in part, sponsored by John Cragg and completed in 1816 at a cost of £12,000. At St Philip's, the brickwork was covered with a layer of stucco, which was reported to be so thin as to barely conceal the joints of the brickwork beneath it. Extensive use was made of cast iron for window frames and tracery, the octagonal turrets, the crockets and other decorations.

Rickman was born in 1776 at Maidenhead where his father was a surgeon and apothecary, and a locally prominent Quaker, a faith to which Thomas, his son, clung for most of his life. In 1807, Rickman moved to Liverpool, working as clerk in an insurance office. His enthusiasm for the Gothic style manifested itself and in co-operation with James Smith, a publisher, Rickman wrote an essay on the architecture of Chester Cathedral (1817) and began the preparation of his An Attempt to Discriminate the Styles of English Architecture. The book proved hugely popular and ran to seven editions, the last in 1881. It was in this book that Rickman coined the well-known names for the periods of medieval architecture – Norman, Early English, Decorated and Perpendicular. Rickman opened an architectural practice in 1819 in Liverpool with a nationwide clientele. In 1821, on being commissioned to design the church of St George in Birmingham, he transferred his main practice to that city, leaving his brother in charge of the Liverpool office. Rickman continued a successful career working on churches and houses until his death in 1841.

Through most of his life, Thomas Rickman adhered to the Quaker faith but, was for a time, attracted to the Catholic Apostolic (Irvingite) Church, a sect which subsequently made use of St Philip's. The founder of this sect, Edward Irving (1792–1834), was a deposed Presbyterian minister who propagated a belief in 'manifestations of the spirit', which included speaking in tongues, prophecy, healing and even raising the dead. Orthodox in other beliefs, it was the organisation of the church in which it diverged from established norms. The church was led by six 'Apostles', chosen by Irving, the last of whom died in 1909.

The church of St Philip in Hardman Street was closed for worship in 1882 but the building went through a series of incarnations, at one stage being a dance hall. The endowments of the church were transferred to a new parish and building – St Philip in Sheil Road. The old building was eventually demolished and a new structure built on the site. Fragments of the iron work of St Philip's can still be seen in its replacement block built on the site of the churchyard.

Thomas Rickman 1776–1841
Rickman was a prominent architect who practised in Liverpool. He was a pioneer of the Gothic Revival and the constructional use of cast iron in buildings. His An Attempt to Discriminate the Styles of English Architecture introduced the familiar names for the periods of medieval building.

A south west view of Trinity Church, Liverpool

Trinity Church was probably the last survivor of the churches depicted by Brierley. After war damage, the church was reopened and rededicated in 1950 and continued in use until 1968 when a reorganisation of parishes and clergy in the city centre led to its closure and demolition in the following year. Trinity Church stood with its west front on the eastern side of St Anne Street and was flanked and isolated by Springfield and what was then known as King Street Soho. The whole area has been transformed by the creation of the Islington dual carriageway which encroaches on the site of Trinity Church.

Trinity had its origins in a petition made by the friends of the Reverend Richard Formby, the squire of Formby and a respected churchman. He had an unequalled reputation for piety and his service to the community, especially for his care of shipwrecked sailors, for which he was honoured with the Freedom of Liverpool. The group of patrons was led by Mr Harvey and Mr Wain. Members of the Harvey family were soap makers, brewers and lime burners – they actually owned the kilns in Lime Street. On 6 July 1791, the Corporation was petitioned to make stone available from the civic quarries 'to complete the Church', which would indicate that building work had already begun. To encourage the generosity of the Council, the plans were submitted but no architect's name is recorded. There were the usual discussions with the Rectors of Liverpool, an arrangement made for the tithes and fees, and a report was prepared for Parliament. The Bill of 26 April 1792 included provision for the erection of a steeple upon the tower and a contract was made with Peter Grant and Company, who had submitted the lowest tender for building a spire at a cost of £340, 'including the materials, vane etc.'

However, there seem to have been doubts about the wisdom of such a spire and a report was commissioned in June 1792, which reported unfavourably on the grounds that the tower was not sufficiently strong to take the weight. The report was signed by John Hope and John Foster the younger. The steeple plan was abandoned, and Trinity had to make do with the square tower with an octagonal upper stage, as seen in this picture.

Behind the eastern end of the church in Brierley's picture can be seen a large residential terrace, known as Trinity Row. In 1808, the middle pedimented house was the scene of an event that provoked a great deal of comment. It was occupied by Charles Angus, a widowed doctor (and, according to some accounts, slave trader), and his sister-in-law, Margaret Burns. In March 1808, Margaret complained of being unwell and suffering an excessive thirst and vomiting. During her sickness she was well taken care of by Angus who sat up with her throughout the night and the following day and night. On 25 March, Margaret Burns said she felt much better. The servant was dispatched to obtain some Madeira she had asked for. On the maid's return, she found Angus asleep in a chair and Margaret Burns dead. Gossip suggested that the two were having an affair, that she had become pregnant and that her illness was the result of poison. Angus was arrested and taken for trial at Lancaster, where some of the greatest forensic talent took part in the trial. The case of the prosecution proved to be weak. The trial attracted much attention and provoked fierce arguments between the medical witnesses called. The evidence was inconclusive and Charles Angus was found not guilty.

West Derby Workhouse, Low Hill, 1830

The administration of the Poor Law was a constant thorn in the side of local administration in the early nineteenth century. The system of 1601 had been intended for use in rural, agricultural parishes but was ill-suited to deal with the increasing urban districts. West Derby, the largest community in the district in early feudal days, found itself surpassed by the growth of Liverpool. The township was developing as a suburb in the shadow of its larger neighbour.

One of the optional courses of action for any parish – in the north of England the term parish was interpreted as the civil township and not the ecclesiastical division – was the establishment of a poorhouse or workhouse for the accommodation and employment of the indigent, a practice encouraged by Knatchbull's Act of 1737 which empowered the parish to refuse relief to paupers who were unwilling to enter the workhouse. West Derby's workhouse is recorded in 1731 but this may not have operated continuously, as it is not listed in a survey of 1777, when Allerton, Childwall and Wavertree were recorded as having workhouses, each with between fifty and sixty inmates.

Liverpool remained a single parish organisation but the ring of outer suburban villages and rural areas was combined into the West Derby Union with 23 constituent parishes from Crosby in the north to Garston in the south, with, according to the 1831 census, a population of 53,058. This organisation was administered by a Board of Guardians with 31 members. This Union was confirmed in its existence by the reforms made to the Poor Law in 1834.

This new organisation needed greatly increased workhouse accommodation and, by 1840, a new building on Mill Road had been built, with beds for 690 inmates and separate accommodation for the mentally ill. Later in the nineteenth century, new workhouses were built at Walton and Toxteth Park for the northern and southern areas of the Union and a substantial administrative building was erected on Brougham Terrace, where the central block still carries the name of the West Derby Union. It is worth remembering that, although the Union Workhouse of the mid-Victorian years was often regarded with dread and apprehension, it played an important part in the development of the district general hospitals. Some of these new infirmaries were located in the old buildings and, until recently, played a vital part in the health care of Liverpool's inner suburbs.

The West Derby Workhouse shown in the illustration is the original building of 1731, with later additions. It was located on Low Hill near to the Coach and Horses public house. The buildings shown in the rear are probably the workshops allocated to the paupers who were expected to earn their keep, if they were physically capable of doing so.

This undated drawing by Brierley represents the last days of the old parish workhouses. By 1834, the Poor Law Amendment Act was passed, requiring measures to be taken to make the administration more efficient and cost effective. One of the most important provisions was the compulsory formation of Poor Law Unions by which parishes and townships came together in a bond, thus reducing administrative duplication and costs, and, it was hoped, making it easier to enforce a regime that, while sustaining life, would not encourage the necessitous to seek aid.

When Liverpool was confined to the peninsula between the Mersey and the Pool, the main route of access to the rest of Lancashire and of the country was along the road which led to the valley or dale of the Pool stream, and then climbed over the heath towards Prescot and Warrington. Although initially a track suitable for equestrian, pack horse and pedestrian traffic, it was the route developed by the turnpike road to Prescot of 1726. The road to Warrington was completed in 1760, linking to the national network. The turnpike only began outside the boundary of the town, at the top of London Road; but street improvements in Liverpool encouraged the gradual development of wheeled traffic and in 1753, a stage-coach service offering the conveyance of passengers and light goods between Liverpool and London was initiated. The journey from the capital started on Friday morning from the Swan with Two Necks and arrived on the following Monday evening at its destination, the Golden Lion, in Dale Street.

By the time Brierley was recording, Liverpool was at the heart of a network of routes used by the mail coaches, whose primary purpose was the delivery of post, but which carried, with speed and regularity, a limited number of passengers. The post office was located in School Lane, close to where the Athenaeum now stands. A more comprehensive passenger service was provided by stage coaches which were designed for the transport of people and parcels, their standards of speed, punctuality and fares being lower than those of the mail coaches. The Directory of 1829 shows that mail coaches were providing a service to Birmingham, Bolton, Blackburn, Chester, Holyhead, and Hull, through York. In addition, coaches ran to give a frequent service to London, Manchester, Whitehaven and the North. There were also regular stage-coach services from the Crown, Golden Lion, Saracen's Head, the Talbot and the Wellington Arms, as well as the Angel, from where the coaches of George Ellwood operated routes to Carlisle and Bristol, with many intermediate stops.

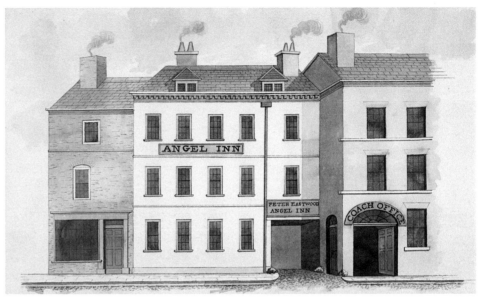

The Angel Inn, Dale Street, 1830.

Because of its status as the principal entrance to the town, Dale Street, in 1830, was well provided with hostelries; several of these were chosen by Brierley as subjects for his drawings. Almost opposite the George, the Angel stood on the corner of John Street with its yard on the west side running at right angles to Dale Street. The Golden Lion was on the south side of the street, on the site subsequently occupied by Queen Building. Its yard, much used by both the mail and stage coaches, is now covered by Queen Street. Other inns located in the area were the Bull Inn, kept by Anne Orrell, on the corner of Truman Street, the Swan Inn, located just to the west of Sir Thomas Street, while in Castle Street the Liverpool Arms was located on the north side, on the corner of Sweeting Street. In addition to these establishments there was a number of other inns and taverns: the Bull and Punch Bowl stood next to the distillery of Mr Houghton in Truman Street, and, nearby was the Mitre, the only one of these inns which still remains, though in a much rebuilt form.

The White Bear, Dale Street, 1830.

From earlier times, the Dale Street inns, especially the Golden Lion and the Fleece, were associated with depots for the pack horse trains. It is easy to forget that the rather more romantic stage coaches were backed by a full service of stage wagons, which carried passengers, as well as goods, on specified routes and the carriers, whose carts served both the locality and more distant towns, carried parcels and passengers. Amongst these was one operated by the well-known firm of Pickford and Company, which had diversified from its initial business in canal transport to operate land-based carrier services from its office in Harrington Street. The inn most noteworthy for its involvement with coaches was the Saracen's Head of Thomas Latham, located between Cumberland Street and Temple Lane, a situation which allowed coaches to enter the yard from Whitechapel and leave by the arch into Dale Street. The Directory of 1829 shows that the Saracen's Head handled most of the mail

coaches, as well as providing a stage-coach service – with a coach known as the Tally Ho! – to London via Birmingham and the West Midlands. From the same inn services also set out to the North and the North East. Coaches for Warrington and Manchester – the Beehive or the Red Rover – left the Saracen's Head 11 times a day. That coaches did not offer the greatest comfort can be judged from the name of the Liverpool–Cheltenham coach, officially the Hirondelle but universally known as the Iron Devil. In the smaller of Brierley's depictions of the Angel, a coach can be discerned standing in the yard. This appears not to be a stage coach but a two-horse post-chaise, perhaps privately owned or available for hire at the larger hotels.

One of the earliest coach proprietors to be successful in Liverpool was Thomas Simpson. His coaches, from the Talbot Inn, linked Liverpool to London, Birmingham, Bristol and Bath, as well as Warrington and Manchester. In turn, Simpson's was later absorbed by Henry Stantham & Co. who also worked the routes to Manchester, Carlisle and Scotland. Stantham's business was taken over by the most successful of the Liverpool coach proprietors, the Bretherton brothers, Bartholomew, Francis and Peter. At the height of their success, they had coaches running from the White Horse, the Saracen's Head and the Angel in Dale Street, where the stables were located, the Crown in Red Cross Street, and the Talbot in Water Street. The name Bretherton, associated with coaching, first appears in both Gore's and Schofield's Liverpool directories of 1800. The situation is confusing but it is evident that they were just becoming involved with the coach trade. Gore's Directory lists Bartholomew and Peter as coach proprietors based at the Crown Inn; however the same two names are recorded as victuallers in a shop at 147 Dale Street. Schofield's Directory for the same year lists Bartholomew as a shop keeper at 89 Dale Street, Peter as a shop keeper at No. 147 and makes no mention of coaches. A study of the directories allows us to chart the brothers' rise to prosperity. Gore's Directory of 1829 contains references to three Brethertons, all now listed as coach proprietors. Bartholomew resided at Rainhill in the house now known as Loyola Hall, a clear demonstration of his increased prosperity. Francis had a house at Lydiate and operated his business from the Crown in Red Cross Street.

The Golden Lion Inn & the Old Public House adjoining, Dale Street, 1828

The third member of the triumvirate, Peter, lived at Parr, St Helen's, and had his headquarters in the Golden Lion in Dale Street. It may be that the Brethertons obtained their coaches from a member of the family, as a coachbuilder of that name is listed with his works on Lime Street. In 1849, Bartholomew is listed in Gore's Directory as 'Gentleman, Rainhill'. He had become a leading figure in the village, having bought the Lordship of the Manor, and founded the Roman Catholic church of St Bartholomew, appropriately sited on the coach road to Warrington.

As the demand for stage-coach travel declined in the face of the spreading railway network, the emphasis of the business shifted to the provision of omnibus services, and, by 1848, members of the Bretherton family were running services between Seaforth, Bootle and Liverpool. This work brought them into contact with Steven Towers, the proprietor of the Waterloo Hotel on Crosby Seabank, some six miles north of the town of Liverpool. The Waterloo Hotel was a popular place of resort for sea bathing and it eventually

gave its name to the district of Waterloo. About 1830, Towers began running a twice-daily horse-drawn omnibus service from the Waterloo which terminated at the Angel Inn, Dale Street. By 1833, Towers had moved from Waterloo and become the proprietor of the Angel. The Hotel, as it had now become, was rebuilt after the original building, depicted by Brierley, had been demolished to make way for Queen Building. The illustration from Towers' advertisement in Gore's Directory of 1834 shows the new hotel, situated on the corner of Dale Street and Castle Street. The new building retained many classical features but was much enlarged and could offer 'A spacious Coffee room, elegant Sitting rooms and Bed Rooms, contiguous baths etc'. The picture shows both an omnibus and a private coach and four to illustrate the

The Angel Inn, Dale Street, 1830.

genteel clientele who might be expected there. Faced by his responsibilities, Towers abandoned the coaching business, but his operations were taken up by a member of the Bretherton family who ran the service under Towers' name. The Brethertons also diversified their investments and Bretherton's Buildings in John Street were erected on the site of their former stable block. It is said that the horse's head decoration on the Tunnel ventilating shaft, which in turn replaced Bretherton's Building, was inspired by this history.

The pictures of Brierley show the contrast between the old-fashioned inns and taverns as represented by the Nag's Head, a building which is probably of late seventeenth-century date, with its distinctive shutters, usually painted in red, its sign of grapes and barrels, and an air of homeliness, in sharp contrast to the elegance of the Golden Lion next door. A supplementary source of income for the Nag's Head was derived from the coach booking office located in one room. It was customary, when reserving a place, to pay half the cost on booking and the remainder when on the coach. Similar in age and status is the White Bear, another of the Dale Street Inns depicted by Brierley and located at 35 Dale Street. Its landlord in 1829 was William Wilson who had succeeded George Taylor as licensee.

Brierley's paintings of the Golden Lion, where the host was Peter Sharples, demonstrate the modern luxury of the good coaching inn at this time. Apart from the rather amiable looking lion on its projecting bracket, the building displays little sign of its commercial purpose. Rather it resembles the house of a substantial city gentleman, built some fifty years before Brierley recorded it and the whole building is designed to give an impression of affluent elegance. Architecturally, the same can be said for the Angel (the proprietor at the time was Peter Eastwood), which Brierley chose to depict twice. Though later absorbed into the Bretherton empire, when the painting was made, the coaches operating out of the Angel were those of George Ellwood and Company. The Directory of 1829 shows that this company provided services to towns of the North and North East, as well as to Hull, Chester and Holyhead, with connections to Shrewsbury, Birmingham and Bristol, as well as London. Ellwood's coach office can be seen to the right of the archway leading to the yard of the Angel in the larger drawing. In that drawing, the small premises shown next door had been the 'Commercial Eating House' of Benjamin Maxwell; perhaps his food was below standard as, by 1829, he seems to have been trading as a cabinet maker in Silkhouse Lane.

A view of old buildings, Dale Street, from Temple Street to Princes Street, 1830

Another picture of an inn located in Dale Street is included in this view. To the centre right of the picture is the Horse and Jockey public house, No. 77 Dale Street, which was kept in both 1825 and 1829 by John Webster. The other buildings provoke some intriguing questions. At first glance, their uses and occupants seem obvious. We have Mayor's the fishmonger, except that this is not recorded in any directory. In 1829 Thomas Mayor kept a provision merchants shop at No. 165 Dale Street, while Baines' Directory of 1825 lists this property, No. 76, as the premises of John Jackson, clog, boot and shoemaker. By 1829, Jackson had removed to No. 109 in the same street. The shop at No. 75 at the time of Brierley's drawing was clearly occupied by 'Jones's Eating House' but, in 1825, this building was the workshop of Joseph Bissel, a cabinet maker and broker. In the Directory for 1829, two possible men named Jones involved in eating houses – today we would call them restaurants – are William Jones, whose establishment was located at 164 Dale Street, and a Richard Jones, who is described as 'commercial eating house proprietor' of No. 8 Charlotte Street. The building displayed in the view might be linked to either of these and represents a very temporary phase in these businesses. The one firm that stays static during this time is at No. 77, to the right of the Horse and Jockey, where in 1825 Martin Nowland had his premises as a quill and feather dresser, though it would seem, judging by the sign displayed, that by 1829 he had added a hairdressing business.

One of the areas of redevelopment which changed the face of Dale Street was the building of what was called The Temple. This was the name given to the area of Temple Street, Temple Lane and Temple Court, a building project of the second half of the eighteenth century which centred on a dissenting chapel, opened in 1763. The new chapel was founded by fractious dissenters who had seceded from the main chapels in Benn's Gardens and Key Street. The chapel, known as the Octagon, was under the leadership of Thomas Bentley, a man who was to be heavily involved in the business development of Josiah Wedgwood. The Octagon Chapel fell out of use and was bought by a member of the Plumbe family who was the Rector of Aughton, to be used as an Anglican chapel, dedicated to St Catherine. The chapel was demolished in 1820 and the whole area absorbed by office buildings, especially the one designed in c.1860 by J. A. Picton on behalf of the banker Sir William Brown and known as 'The Temple'.

The Athenaeum, Church Street, 1830

The second half of the eighteenth century saw a cultural flowering in Liverpool. The town, once dominated by the demands of commerce, now began to assume a cultural mantle that was compared to Renaissance Florence. The Royal Institution, the Liverpool Library and Lyceum, the Botanic Gardens and the Liverpool Academy of Arts replaced the Unanimous Society and the Ugly Face Club as places of resort for the urban mercantile prince. There was a demand for a place where party political and religious divisions were set aside and men could meet to exchange news and gossip, to study and to socialise on equal and non-partisan terms. The Athenaeum project began in 1797 with a meeting of William Roscoe, Dr Currie and some of their associates, mainly of an abolitionist, reformist and Non-conformist cast of mind. Soon the subscription list was filled with men of many and varied attitudes; as a catalogue of the library, published in 1864, puts it, 'men of all shades of opinion, political and religious, concurred with equal zeal in promoting the success of an institution designed to facilitate the acquisition of knowledge'. The most important facility provided by the Athenaeum for the dissemination of knowledge was the excellent members' library in which 25,000 books were available for consultation. When John Foster was commissioned in 1798 to design premises for the new Athenaeum, he had two priorities. He had to provide an adequate and well-illuminated newsroom where the newspapers and commercial gazettes would be available for the perusal of the Proprietors. This was also the main social room.

His second objective was to house the library in a suitable room.

The site of the original Athenaeum building faced onto Church Street, near to the entrance to Church Alley. To the right, the Athenaeum was flanked by the house of Mr George Case, a prominent merchant, active in the town's affairs who was deeply involved in the creation of the Athenaeum. To the right of Case's house, standing on the corner of Church Street and Church Alley, was the Dispensary, founded in 1778 to provide health care for the sick who could not afford medical advice and who had been recommended by a patron or one of the local magistrates. To the left of the Athenaeum building was the saleroom of Thomas Wynstanley and Son who were auctioneers and valuers, specialising in fine works of art.

George Case

George Case was a member of a family heavily involved in the life of Liverpool. A nephew of Sarah Clayton, he traded as a merchant, became mayor in 1781 and served on the Council for 57 years. He was a receiver of taxes for Liverpool and played an important part in organising the defences of the town to confront any French invasion. His house, until he removed to Walton Priory, was next door to the Athenaeum in Church Street. [Athenaeum Proprietor No. 475]

J. A. Picton, himself an architect, as well as an historian, says of the Athenaeum façade: 'The design, though unpretending is not devoid of character and merit. Its principal fault is a degree of flatness and feebleness in the details' – a severe case of damning with faint praise. There is, however, a certain justice in his evaluation of the building as shown in Brierley's picture. The very conventional frontage had a rusticated, lower storey and large arched windows, intended to provide good daylight in the newsroom. The first floor was provided with some unconvincing 'Greek' decoration that appears to have been added as an afterthought to conform to the conventions of the day. The upper floor was part of the Library which had a central well with a balcony and shelves at third floor level

The original Athenaeum building was in use until 1924. At that time the Corporation was anxious to widen Church Street and eventually the Proprietors agreed to remove their premises to Church Alley. A new building, designed by Harold Dod, was opened in 1928. It is still the present home of the institution. A fuller and more detailed description of the Athenaeum and its library can be found on page 24.

A view of old buildings, Bath Street, 1830

These examples of Brierley's drawings show the two blocks of buildings which lay on the landward side of Bath Street, between Queen Street and Brook Street, and intersected by Barton Lane. Brook Street was named for Mr Joseph Brooks, owner of the land which had previously been used for a brick field. The period of development can be related to the reign of Queen Anne by the street names: Queen Street, Union Street – commemorating the Act of Union between England and Scotland 1707 – and Gibraltar Row, commemorating the capture of the Rock in 1704. However, little building occurred until the nineteenth century, as street maps of Brierley's period show large empty spaces and just a fringe of building. Two of the early eighteenth-century buildings shown appear to be intended for use as factories or workshops with wide tunnel entrances, capable of taking a loaded dray into the yard. One of the buildings also has a long, workshop-style window, a type common in buildings devoted to hand-loom weaving or skilled mechanical working which required a good light.

Two of the buildings are public houses. Both look as though they might have been some of the earliest buildings constructed on Bath Street and may indeed be the first development of the area. The rustication and false keystones of the window lintels are a good indication of an early eighteenth-century date. On the corner of Queen Street and Bath Street stands the Cross Keys, identifiable by its sign. It also has a painted sign for Old Cumberland House. In 1825, the Cross Keys was kept by Martha Williams. Next door is a house, which appears to be of an earlier style, simply labelled Parr's, but its carved sign has a crown which confirms that its full name was the Rose and Crown, kept in 1824 by James Parr. Something of a mystery surrounds Hamer's Wines. No business of that name anywhere in Liverpool is recorded in the directories, except for a Joseph Hamer, wine and spirit dealer of Great Crosshall Street in 1821. The name Old Cumberland House, so prominently painted on the wall, is also absent from the directories and no public house of that name appears in the lists.

The name Bath Street has its origins in the presence of a bathing establishment on its seaward side. Liverpool and the Lancashire coast seem to have had a tradition of sea bathing that can be traced long before the date usually ascribed to the vogue, following the treatment of George III. That Liverpool may have shared in this vogue is suggested by evidence drawn from the Buck Brothers' engraving A South West Prospect of Liverpool, where an isolated building stands on the water's edge on the shore at the northern fringe of the town. There are suggestions that this represents a 'Bathing House'.

This print gives us a good idea of the topography of this area, with grassy slopes from the north end of Old Hall Street terminating in low, clay cliffs, some of which had been enclosed behind the embankment of the New Quay, the northern end of which was Bath Street. What remains unclear is if this name predates the opening – in about 1765, by Mr John Wright – of a bathing establishment at this point. A full description of the baths and their facilities is given in *Liverpool As It Was 1775–1800* by Richard Brooke [Liverpool Libraries and information Services 2003 p.409].

In 1794, the Corporation took over the baths, and improved the facilities. In 1817, the baths were demolished to make way for the construction of Prince's Dock, and replaced by the 'Floating Bath' moored in the river. A Herdman print of the floating bath is outside the Dining Room of the Athenaeum. It looks singularly dank and forbidding. In 1826, a new baths building was erected by the Corporation on St George's Parade, a building prominent in views of the waterfront.

Picture 1

This picture shows the block of Hanover Street between the end of Manesty Lane and Peter Lane. It gives a good impression of the very mixed nature of both the architecture and the occupancy of the street. The imposing building on the corner of Manesty Lane is the Shropshire Tavern, whose landlord in 1825 was Thomas Owen. Several public houses in Liverpool were named after distant areas or towns. The names possibly commemorated the places from which their proprietors originally came and may also have attracted customers from those places who could meet people from the same locality. The double fronted and elegant building in the centre is the old Excise Office, formerly the Heywoods' house. The Office was replaced with new premises between Fleet Street and Gradwell Street. In 1825, the former Excise building contained the offices of John Roberts, a merchant, David Lythgoe, a corn merchant, and T. Robinson & Co., general merchants.

Picture 2

In this picture, Hanover Street to the east of Peter Lane is shown. The first block on the left is the bow-fronted building, prefigured in Picture 1, the premises of Joseph Burley & Co., drysalters. The term drysalter was used for dealers in chemical products including glue, varnish and dye stuffs for domestic or commercial use. The adjacent building, with its integral warehouse, was in multiple occupancy and contained the premises of A. Hunter, tobacco merchant, two offices of general merchants, those of G. Campbell, Aspinall, Brown & Aspinall, Edward Blackmore and John Swainston who were two firms of shipping brokers. The house next door, with its pedimented door case and railings, was run as a boarding house by Mrs Sarah Ray.

Picture 3

This continues the panorama of Hanover Street commencing on the left with the premises of Andrew Nairn, a wine and porter merchant. Adjacent, at No. 20, was the office of Thomas Avison's practice as an attorney and notary public. Despite the building's residential appearance Avison lived in Upper Islington. The adjoining house was the home of John Lloyd, the Port Gauger. A Gauger was an official employed by the Custom service to examine bulk cargoes and particularly to test the capacity of casks. The building with the sign Neesham's was a public house, the landlady being Mrs Elizabeth Neesham.

Picture 4

John Clarke, the plumber and painter, lived at 120 London Road and the premises in 24 Hanover Street were used as a shop, stores and workshop. Interestingly, the 1825 Directory lists John Clarke in Hanover Street as plumber, painter and glazier but also a John Clarke as a working jeweller at No. 44 in the same street. It seems unlikely, but not impossible, that the man had two trades.

Picture 5

Horwood's plan of Liverpool (1803) shows a large, empty piece of open ground in Hanover Street, extending from the corner of College Lane towards School Lane. By Brierley's, time this had been enclosed by a wall. In this drawing, the wall is a dominant feature and we can see how John and Joseph Jones, iron merchants, had acquired a portion of the open land and erected a warehouse and shop, with the entrance in College Lane. The building in the background is the gable end of Pool House built, reputedly in 1556, by Alderman Corbett, and had served as the Parish Poor House after the implementation of the Poor Law Act of 1601. However, Picton claims that the building was demolished in 1804 and that Bullock's Museum and Waxworks, one of the great tourist attractions of Liverpool at this period, was erected on the site. This picture appears to contradict this assertion. Perhaps not all the former Poor House was razed to the ground and the gable end was preserved. On the other corner of College Lane were the premises of James Townley. The Directory shows that his public house was officially the Blue Bell and the sign is visible on the corner of the building. Though listed in 1825 as a victualler, by 1829 he had diversified his activities and was described as 'Joiner, cabinet maker and victualler'.

Picture 6

The buildings shown in this picture extend from Jones' walled yard [see above] almost to School Lane. They present an interesting and varied usage. At No. 32, Hannah Bailey carried on her trade as an upholsterer and next door Maria Wood worked as a silk grafter – one who either joined silk threads or who mixed silk and other fibres. At No. 38 William Mossman was a dealer in tea and flour while next door to him James Appleton was a hairdresser and perfumier. Adjacent to him was a tavern and oyster house. Oysters were a very popular dish and consumed in huge quantities at this time, mostly by the working class.

Picture 7

There appears to be a break in the panorama of Hanover Street at this point. Horwood's map shows an open space which had been in-filled by 1824, though it may be that it is hinted at by the left-hand margin of the drawing, where the gable end of the building can be seen. The left-hand house was occupied by Margaret Austin, a teacher, while the other two properties were the offices of a firm of attorneys, Keightley and Son. Next door to them was the shop of Dunbar Gibson, a shoe-maker, whose residence was at 25 Fairhurst Street.

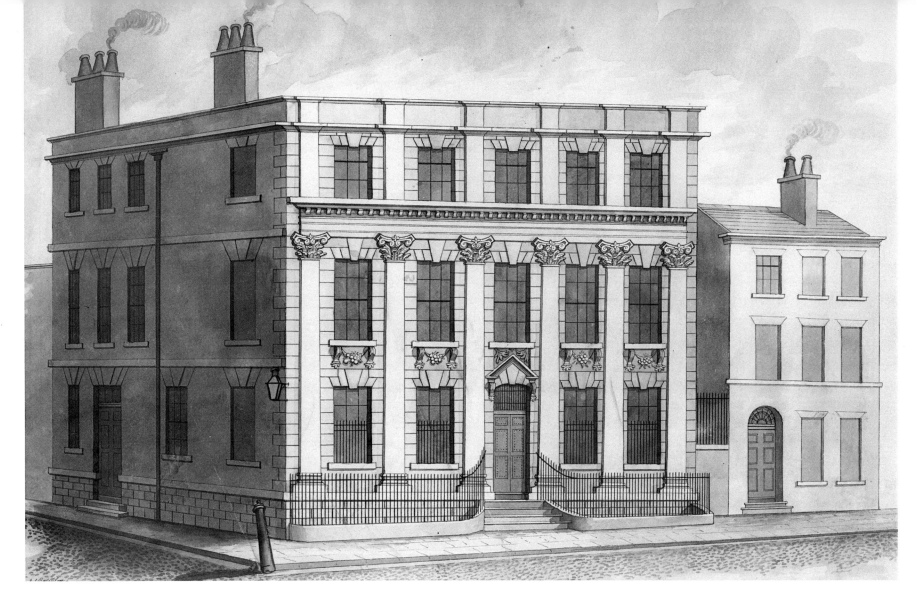

Picture 8

This imposing house, formerly in the possession of the Steers family, has an interesting history. It embodies most of the features which might be expected of an early Georgian house, stone built, an elaborate door case with pediment, a façade divided into six bays by Corinthian pilasters and with a dentil cornice. In about 1769, the house was bought by Mr Thomas Seel, a wealthy merchant. At the rear of the house was a large garden which extended as far as the present line of Colquitt Street. In 1827, the Bank of England extended its activities by setting up provincial branches and it was Seel's house in Hanover Street which was purchased as a temporary establishment in Liverpool.

Picture 9

This block which extended from Fleet Street to the corner of Seel Street is now occupied by the Hanover Hotel and a variety of other shops. Little information is available about the establishments shown here which appear to be purpose-built office accommodation, with some form of central hall or atrium. The name Hanover Rooms does not appear in any directory of the period. The Bank of England building (see above) is visible on the right-hand margin.

A view of Christ Church, Hunter Street, Liverpool, 1830

Christ Church, located two hundred yards from Trinity Church, is another example of the way in which disputes on theology and practice bedevilled the churches of Liverpool. There were sufficient wealthy patrons in the town to indulge their predilections by the endowment of churches which were little more than private chapels. Mr John Houghton was a prosperous distiller and rectifier of spirits, whose business premises were at the junction of Trueman Street and Dale Street and still survive, though bizarrely interrupted by the art-deco frontage of the Mitre public house. As was typical in the period, he also had his home adjacent to his works and offices. The elegant house (c.1790) survives to this day. The frontage in Trueman Street is of four storeys, with a three bay pediment. A Venetian window with decoration in the Adam style is on the first floor over the front door. The door case, in turn, is decorated with pilasters and a fanlight with tracery; it is probably the most elaborate surviving Georgian house in Liverpool.

It seems likely that when Houghton decided to build a church, where the theology and practice would meet his requirements, he employed the architect of his house to design Christ Church. There is a remarkable similarity in the two buildings, particularly in the details of the central Venetian window of the frontage of the church and in the false balustrades beneath the flanking lights. The church was built of brick and the wooden dome with its decorated louvered roundel and cupola seems to be lead covered. The cost of the building was variously recorded as £15,000 [Memorials of Liverpool J. A. Picton] and £22,000 [Liverpool As It Was, R. Brooke, Liverpool Libraries 2003]. A novel feature of the interior was that it had double galleries around three sides, though these were subsequently removed. This façade of the building shows that it had a crypt which was entered through the large door with a rusticated arch. The skull and crossbones carved on the keystone indicated that this was intended as a charnel house. Though described as being located in Hunter Street, from which this view has been drawn, the maps show that the church could almost be as well described as in Islington or Christian Street. The windmill in the background was sited on the junction of Islington and Christian Street (see page 99).

Construction of the church began in 1797 and it was consecrated by the Bishop of Chester in 1800. The early history of Christ Church is an excellent example of the heated nature of ecclesiastical politics within Liverpool. It was supposed that Houghton intended to place as incumbent his friend, the popular preacher, Reverend Robert Bannister, whose views coincided with the liberal attitudes of the patron. While the church was being built, the two men quarrelled and the appointment was given to another man. Bannister's friends then raised a subscription and acquired a nearby former tennis court in Grosvenor Street where they built him a church which was dedicated to All Saints. The Reverend Turner, who succeeded Bannister, earned some notoriety when he became involved with the scandalous Bishop West. The religious activity of the period may be praiseworthy but Christian charity and tolerance seem to have been lacking.

A view of the Church for the Blind, Duncan Street East, 1830

Edward Rushton 1756–1814

Educated at the Liverpool Free School, Edward Rushton was apprenticed to the Master of a slave ship. On one occasion his skill and bravery saved the ship when all hope had been abandoned. While treating the slaves suffering from contagious ophthalmia, he contracted the disease and lost the sight of one eye while the other was impaired. After leaving the sea he tried various occupations and became the editor of the Liverpool Herald, in which he made no effort to conceal his radical views. He was instrumental in the establishment of the Liverpool School for the Indigent Blind in 1791.

In the last decades of the eighteenth century, Liverpool was notable for the many charitable organisations it supported. The School for the Blind, founded in 1791, was the first institution of its type in Britain. There is dispute as to the originator of the idea but credit must go to Edward Rushton, whose sight was seriously damaged while a sailor in the slave trade. His experiences gave him a life-long aversion to slavery and he was one of the most vociferous abolitionists in Liverpool. Despite his disability, Rushton opened a printing and book shop in Paradise Street and achieved a reputation as a poet. His works The Dismembered Empire and West Indian Eclogues were well received as passionate statements of the Abolitionist cause.

The original premises for the school were in Commutation Row, between London Road and Islington. After a somewhat uncertain start, the school flourished and, by 1800, a larger building had been constructed on the south side of London Road. The new school provided residential accommodation, workshops and teaching rooms. General education was not neglected but the residents, who were of all ages and both sexes, were taught skills and kept gainfully employed in basket making, spinning and the production of whips. In November 1827, the Athenaeum accounts record that £4 17s. 7d. was spent on a Lobby cloth – probably a floor covering – made by the School for the Blind. The School had a fine reputation for music and singing, largely through the efforts of a blind music teacher, John Christie, who saw music-making as a way in which the blind people could earn a living.

It seems to have been Christie's idea that a chapel, with a high standard of music, would attract a congregation and provide funds for the charity. The chapel was a separate building standing on the opposite side of Duncan Street (later renamed Hotham Street) to the other buildings of the institution and was flanked by Great Nelson and Sidney Streets. An underground passage afforded a safe link between the institution and the chapel. When the building was complete and the chapel dedicated by the Bishop of Chester, on 6 October 1819, it must have been a subject of astonished comment. The architect was John Foster the younger who had recently returned from spending some time in Italy and Greece, in architectural and archaeological investigation with C. R. Cockerell. He had gained a feeling for the ascetic pleasures of Greek architecture. This taste had been encouraged by recent publications, notably Stuart & Revett's Antiquities of Athens. Inspired by the new fashion and what he had seen, Foster provided a design which was the first building of the archaeological Classical revival in Liverpool. Soon the style was to be seen in buildings of all types.

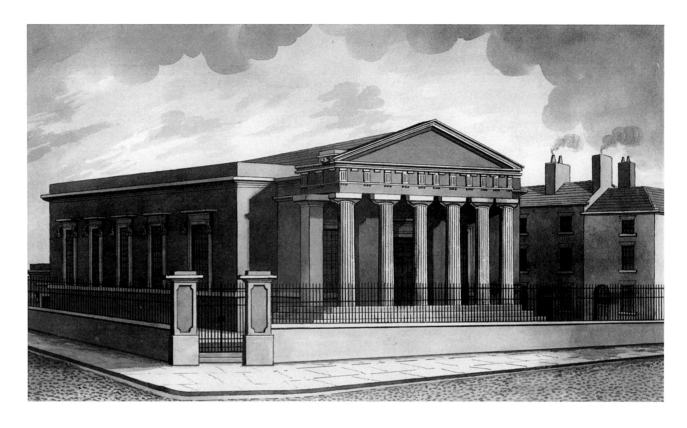

The main part of the structure was a simple rectangular cell pierced with five windows, each with architraves and elaborate cornices. The façade, allegedly based on the design of the Temple of Jupiter Panhellenius on Aegina, had a central door, flanked by a pair of large windows. This surmounted a stylobate of five steps and was crowned with a peristyle of six Doric columns. The architrave is plain and unadorned while the frieze is punctuated by eleven triglyphs, stopped by a dentil cornice which supports the pediment. It is drawn from a textbook of Greek architecture and the only aberration from the classical design is that the main building extends beyond the peristyle. According to contemporary accounts, the chapel was impressive in its original situation and, when the school moved to Hardman Street in 1851, the chapel was transported stone by stone to the new site where it was re-erected.

Globe Chambers, John Street, Late Globe Tavern, 1830

The early nineteenth century saw the development of an important aspect of the built environment of Liverpool: the office block. The merchant or commercial man might be able, as we have seen, to incorporate his office or counting house into the same building as his warehouse and often his dwelling. The professional man, however, did not have the same opportunity and needed to seek chambers for his practice. The construction of the Exchange in 1808, as a speculative business development, had a magnetic effect in drawing the business houses towards it and its surrounding area. At a time when most day-to-day business communication was by word of mouth, a location near to the Exchange was an essential asset. At the same time, it was becoming increasingly common for wealthier men to move to more salubrious suburbs. Consequently, they required office premises in what was becoming the business centre of the town.

It seems that, at this period, a number of Liverpool's older inns were falling out of use, including the Globe Tavern and the King's Arms (see page 163). Some of Liverpool's older inns and taverns were possibly struggling to compete with the new style 'hotel' that was modelled on the French example, providing food and accommodation on a somewhat grander and more luxurious scale. However, the existing buildings with numerous rooms and facilities were eminently suitable for conversion into office accommodation.

John Street was developed as a cul-de-sac off Dale Street in the earlier part of the eighteenth century and only extended as far as Harrington Street. The Globe Tavern was one of the earliest buildings on the street. Its architectural details, notably the console brackets supporting the windowsills and replacing the keystones over the windows, the scrolled pediment over the door case, with its Corinthian pilasters all clearly indicate the style of the last decades of the seventeenth century or the earliest part of the eighteenth.

In 1825, the Globe Chambers, as the old tavern had been renamed, had four different occupiers. William Sedgewick, a Commission Broker (a person who trades in securities on behalf of an investor), was still in his offices in 1829. Robert Atherton practised as an attorney in John Street and lived around the corner at No. 13 in the newly developed Temple Court. By 1829 he had departed both addresses. The third occupant of Globe Chambers was John Farrar, who is described as a 'Ship broker and agent to London traders'. Farrar had premises at Stanton's Wharf and a business in London Road where he traded as hosier. It seems an unlikely combination of activities! Other evidence shows that the hosiery business in London Road was run by a Sarah Farrar, presumably a female relative. Sharing the Globe Chambers was its fourth occupant, Charles Davies, a law stationer who lived on Rose Hill. His business had closed by 1829.

At the time that Brierley was making his picture, John Street was undergoing a radical change. In 1829, a long delayed Corporation project for widening the streets was, at last, put into effect. John Street, together with Lord Street, Cable Street, Trafford Lane and King Street were included in a project budgeted at £106,000 for widening and improving the previously narrow and dark streets. In addition, John Street was extended to intersect with Lord Street from whence the new Marshall Street (now South John Street) continued to the dock. Today, evidence of this improvement work can be found in the elegant Harrington Chambers, a good indication of the architectural quality of the new building along the extended street.

John Street has significance in the cultural history of Liverpool. The Liverpool Library, England's first subscription library, originated in the John Street home of a schoolmaster, Mr William Everard. A number of the intelligentsia of the town would meet there for debate and discussion. About 1758, they began to buy books to stock a library for the members' use. By 1786 the accommodation was inadequate and the library moved to a new building in Lord Street. Later, this collection of books became the nucleus around which the library of the Lyceum was created. It was not a public library but was only open to subscribers and, unusually for the time, would admit ladies.

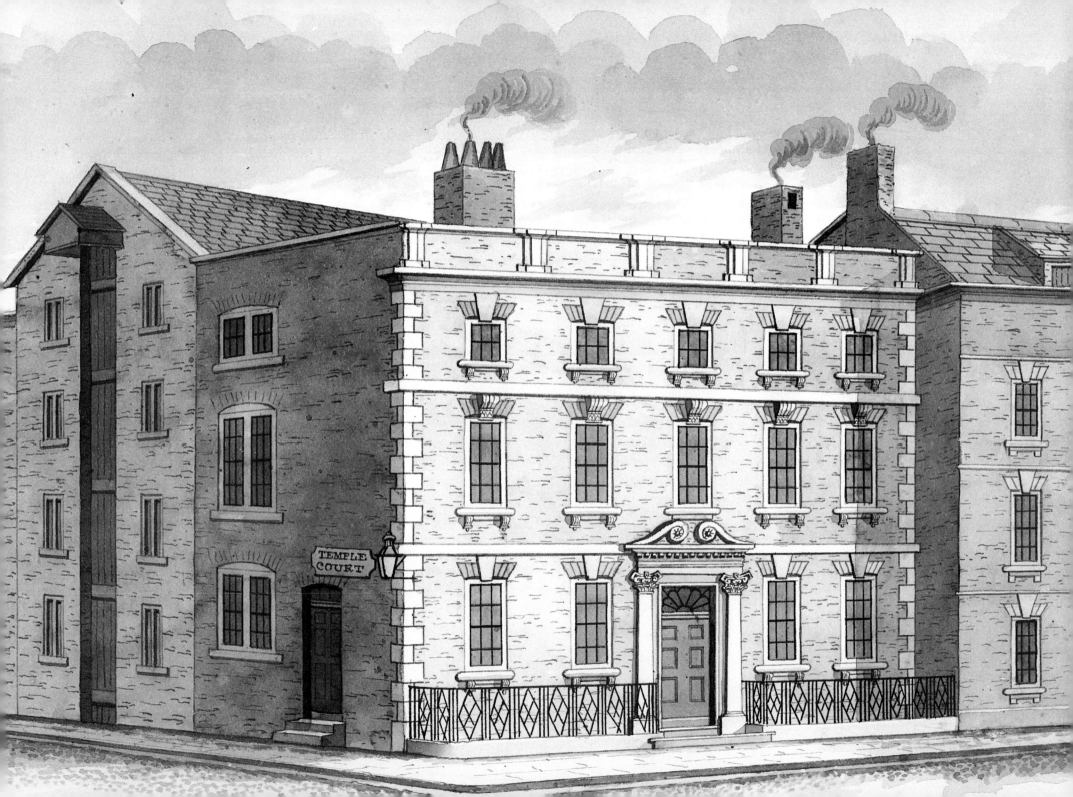

A view of cottages in the old Haymarket and St John's Place, 1828

The development of the area of the Pool Stream valley could not take place until the brook had been culverted and the area artificially drained, which was carried out between 1750 and 1760. The one-time Frog Lane was renamed Whitechapel. A large open area at the east end of Whitechapel was adopted as the hay market. Being on the edge of the town, this site obviated the necessity of the huge haywains, piled high with their loads, negotiating the narrow town streets and was also a convenient destination for wagons from either the east, or from the agricultural areas of south west Lancashire using Scotland Road. Adjacent to the market area on its eastern side was the church of St John (see page 111). According to rumour some of the inhabitants of the street were involved as 'Resurrection Men' in the adjoining churchyard.

The area was defined by a trapezium of streets formed, on the northern side, by Shaw's Brow, with its residential cottages and pot banks. The southern arm was St John's Place, while Lime Street formed the eastern side. The Old Haymarket closed the western extremity. The centre of this plot contained the Infirmary, the Seamen's Hospital and the Lunatic Asylum, together with a large open area of the Infirmary garden and, needless to add, the precinct of St John's Church and its cemetery.

By the early nineteenth century, the Old Haymarket became too small and a new market was set out (1819) at the junction of St John's Lane and Lime Street. Some of this plot was lost on the building of St Georges' Hall but the site is marked by the wide junction that still exists between Lime Street and St John's Lane, opposite to the façade of Lime Street Station. Brierley depicts Rimmington Row, called after the original lessee of that plot of land. The cottages date from the mid years of the eighteenth century when this land was being developed, the long, multi-paned windows on some of the upper floors suggesting the presence, at one time, of workshops requiring extra light. In 1825, there were craftsmen artisans in Old Haymarket. The Danson brothers, for example, were cabinet makers, and at No. 1 Peter Phythian had a shoemaking business. There were two dealers in flour – George Dickson and Thomas Edelston – while Holmes and Son were herring smokers and cudbear-makers, the latter being a purple or violet dye made from an extract of lichen. Thomas Watkinson was a tobacco and snuff dealer and John Milburn was a saddler. Other shops included Williams' tailoring and drapery store, Maria Sutton's haberdashery and Richard Miller's hairdressers and perfumery. The row also had residential tenants, including the curate of St John's, Reverend D. Hewitt at No. 20, and Lieutenant Hughes of the 2nd Royal Lancashire Militia.

In the drawing, the house on the extreme left is the home of George Davey, a book-keeper. Next door to the right is the residence of Lieutenant Hughes and then to the right again is William Jopling's Hay Cart tavern. Next door is another public house, kept by Margaret Harwood, and known as the Machine House, the name perhaps referring to a near-by weighing machine. This public house extends into St John's Place, where the three doors shown are the entrances to the premises of Robert Baldwin, a flour dealer, James Garner, a dealer in small wares, and the office of John Harding, who worked as a Commission Agent and House Broker.

Houses, bottom of Mount Pleasant, opposite Brownlow Hill, 1828

The name Mount Pleasant was of comparatively recent origin when this drawing was made. The grassy hill with its market garden, bowling green and inn had been known for many years as Martindale Hill, after a former keeper of the ale house. About 1760, the name seems to have changed, in popular usage, to become Mount Pleasant. It was here that the young William Roscoe was brought up and worked in his father's inn and market garden at the top of the hill. In the time of James Brierley, Mount Pleasant was still very much on the periphery of the town, an area whose rustic charm had attracted a number of distinguished and wealthy men to build large houses, many of which were set in extensive, landscaped grounds. The residents included Sir George Dunbar, a wealthy broker, William Ewart (1798–1869), the godfather of William Ewart Gladstone, and Rector Roughsedge who held the living of Liverpool from 1796 until 1829 and whose memorial by William Spence can be seen in Liverpool Parish Church. Another resident was John Foster the younger, the architect of so much of Liverpool in this period, whose house is marked by a plaque and now occupied by John Moore's University.

William Ewart 1798–1869
Born in Liverpool, Ewart [Athenaeum Proprietor No. 385] was a highly successful broker but a less successful politician with interests in government reform and social improvement. Ewart lived on Mount Pleasant and later at Wavertree. He was a close friend of John Gladstone and was godfather to Gladstone's fourth son who was baptised William Ewart.

Reverend Robert Hankinson Roughsedge
Robert Roughsedge was one of the Rectors of Liverpool between 1796
and 1829 and was noted for his mild, simple and generous spirit. The son
of Edward Roughsedge, he was educated at Brasenose College, graduating
as M.A. in 1771. He married a Miss Waring of Bury, described as being of
'a respectable family of Redivals.' A fine memorial to Roughsedge, carved
by William Spence, can be found in Liverpool Parish Church.
[Athenaeum Proprietor No. 50]

Brierley shows that not all Mount Pleasant was lined with the residences of 'The Quality' and that, at the lower end, there was a number of small business premises in buildings that dated from the eighteenth century, and which were decorated with classical motifs. The Union Tavern stood at 103 Mount Pleasant, and is marked out in the picture by its hanging barrel sign.

In 1825, it was kept by Thomas Whittaker, though he was a newcomer who is not listed in the Directory for 1821. The architecture of the Union and the building next door seems to reflect a rural origin, with their appearance being reminiscent of a farmhouse of an earlier period. In 1825, the adjacent building to the public house was occupied by John Innes, a baker, who, by 1829, had removed to 88 Mount Pleasant. His next door neighbour was Ellen Hayhurst, a flour dealer, conveniently located to supply Innes' bakery. By 1829 Ellen had not only moved her premises to Pilgrim Street but had changed her occupation, becoming established as a lodging house keeper. The building on the corner of Mount Pleasant and Renshaw Street appears to be of a more modern construction. A faint ghost of this building, rebuilt and re-faced, still survives and was formerly the the University Club and later,shop of Boot's Chemist but is now a cafe bar.

Renshaw Street, named after the Reverend Samuel Renshaw, who was one of the Rectors of Liverpool from 1794 to 1822, originated in a country lane leading towards St James' Mount. Baines' map of 1821 shows it fully built up. The ecclesiastical tone was maintained by the presence of the Unitarian Chapel, built in 1811 and attended by such luminaries as the Rathbone family and William Roscoe, who was interred in the chapel burial ground. Today, a garden and memorial commemorates him. Opposite the Unitarian Chapel was St Andrew's Church (see page 109); while in Oldham Street stood the Scottish Church, opened for Presbyterian worship in 1783. Attached to this church was the Caledonian School, opened in 1812 and providing for 160 boys and 90 girls. The Independent Chapel in Newington was opened by a secessionist group from the Ancient Chapel of Toxteth in 1777. This chapel was sometimes referred to as Newington Bridge Chapel, the development of that street having been hampered by the presence of two rope walks athwart its track. The problem had been overcome by the building of a dry bridge over the roperies. The opening of St Luke's Church (see page 53) completed a remarkable collection of church buildings within a single street.

A view of the Liverpool Theatre, 1825

The theatre was built in 1772 during a time when the whole area of Williamson Square was under development. In 1764, the Williamson family, one of the most distinguished and active in Liverpool affairs, owned a considerable area of land on the east side of Whitechapel and sought permission from the Corporation to pave it and set up a market. The Council gave permission on the understanding that the Williamson family would undertake to fill up a great deal of marshy ground which ran along Frog Lane, now Whitechapel, formerly the valley of the Pool Stream. The market failed to attract trade and the wide piazza became a site for the building of houses for the affluent.

In December 1771, William Gibson, a 'comedian' and Norwich theatre owner petitioned the Mayor and Council of Liverpool for the erection of a playhouse. In support of his application, he cited his experience and the insalubrious nature of the existing theatre in Liverpool's Drury Lane. The Letters Patent were issued by the Lord Chamberlain in February 1770. A subscription list was opened and filled within an hour. With the money raised, building began but before the theatre, named The Theatre Royal, opened in June 1772 its great protagonist died and was buried in the churchyard at Walton. The opening performance comprised the Tragedy of Mahomet and a farce, The Deuce is in Him.

The frontage of the original theatre was simpler than the one shown in this picture. A central pediment contained a carving of the Royal Arms, while a Venetian window formed a centrepiece over the main door. This was flanked by two smaller doors and two windows. The design shown here was the result of an extension of 1802. The neo-classical, curved façade with its paired Ionic pilasters, carved panels and twin doors in the rusticated lower storey of the new building is the one depicted by Brierley.

The theatre re-opened in June the following year with the comedy Speed the Plough. During the decade between 1820 and 1830, the Theatre Royal was attracting some of the premier actors of the period, including Charles Macready and Charles Kemble. An appearance by Sarah Siddons, however, had received a very mixed reaction from the Liverpool audience. Shakespeare's plays were popular and Macbeth, Othello, Hamlet and Richard III were performed. In 1822, the theatre closed for redecoration and refurbishment, and re-opened with a performance of Coriolanus. In the time between these serious plays a whole variety of lighter comedies and farces were enacted. The efforts of the actors were not always appreciated. On being hissed, an actor attacked Liverpool as a place where every stone was cemented by black blood.

Though in its period the most celebrated of the Liverpool theatres, the Royal was by no means the only one. The first dated reference to a theatre in Liverpool comes in 1745 when a company of actors, stranded in the passage to Ireland by bad weather, gave a performance in the cockpit in what was then known as Blackberry Lane (William Street). Inspired by the success of this episode, it is said that a playhouse was built in the Old Ropery near Drury Lane. This small house proved inadequate and a much larger theatre was built in the same place which opened in June 1749. By Brierley's day, there was a number of other theatres in Liverpool. They included The Liver in Church Street, close to the Athenaeum and the Sans Pareil Theatre in Ranleagh Street, where the painted displays, known as Marshall's Moving Panorama were a popular attraction. In 1795, the equestrian Philip Astley, excluded from the Theatre Royal, built a wooden hall in Christian Street, known variously as the Circus, the Queen's Theatre and the Adelphi.

Williamson Square was unusually well supplied with hostelries to enable the audience of the theatre to obtain refreshment, before, during or after a performance. On the corner of Tarleton Street stood the York Hotel of James Galloway, who had succeeded Ellen Crowther, the hostess of 1825. Next to the theatre, two public houses occupied Nos 8 and 9. In the former, John Marshall ran a tavern which bore his name, while next door Ann Lettman

The civic activities of Moses Benson would seem to illustrate the hypocrisy which is charged against the Liverpool slave merchants. He was a member of the Vestry and shared in their responsibility for the care of the poor. In 1786, he was one of the first to make a contribution to the fund for the building of a lunatic asylum. In 1803, he was amongst those appointed to raise money for the building of a fort to protect the entrance to the port of Liverpool. He served as Colonel of a regiment of volunteer Light Horse and, when he died, part of the pleasure gardens of his house was allocated for the site of a new church for the 'Lower Orders' – St Michael's in Pitt Street.

On the death of Elizabeth Kent, the house in Duke Street was purchased by Moses Benson, another of the leading merchants of Liverpool. Benson had been born in Lancashire in 1738, but went to sea and later settled in the West Indies, where he amassed a considerable fortune. On his return, he bought a country estate at Lutwyche in Shropshire but established his Liverpool base in the house in Duke Street, where he seems to have spent most of his time. As we have seen before, it was also his business headquarters from which he conducted the affairs of Benson and Sons, in partnership with two of his sons.

At the centre of his business empire was his interest in the slave trade. The records of his slave voyages show, that between 1784 and 1806, Benson was part owner of vessels on 84 different voyages. The records also show that over 200 slaves were embarked on each voyage. Benson was, therefore, responsible for transporting over 24,000 Africans for the slave trade.

The streets and buildings surrounding St Peter's Church, 1828–1830

Old Houses, Hanover Street, corner of Manesty Lane, 1828

Perhaps no area of the city centre has undergone as much change as that depicted by Brierley in this series of drawings. It is more difficult today to relate to the topography that he shows here than in any other part of the town, following the total alteration and enclosure of streets in the immense Liverpool One development. This area, in Brierley's day, was a triangle formed by Hanover Street, Church Street and Paradise Street and was intersected by two principal streets running east and west, School Lane and College Lane,

and these in turn were crossed by two north–south orientated roads, Peter's Lane and Manesty Lane.

The area was dominated by three buildings, St Peter's Church, consecrated in August 1704, which lay at about the midpoint on the Church Street side of the triangle with an east–west orientation. The architecture of the church was uninspired and its architect unknown, though a strong case can be made for it having been designed by John Moffat. The principal glory of the church was the superb woodcarving by Richard Prescot. Some examples of his work survived the demolition of the church in 1922 and can be seen in St Cuthbert's, Churchtown and St Stephen's, Banks. The churchyard was flanked to the east by Church Alley and on the west by Church Lane.

The second principal building within the triangle was the Bluecoat Hospital, now known as Bluecoat Centre for Modern Art. In 1708, one of the Rectors, Robert Styth, and the wealthy sea captain and merchant Bryan Blundell, became concerned about the plight of the orphans who thronged the streets. They established a day school near St Peter's and employed a Master at £20 per annum. After several uncertain years, Blundell, in 1713, placed the establishment on a sounder financial basis and acquired a new site on which the building was raised. Again, the architect is unknown but Thomas Ripley and Thomas Steers have both been suggested. The boys were taught '… to read, write and cast accounts', while the girls were instructed in 'knitting and housewifery'. Both sexes, as the inscribed frieze which decorates the front of the building tells us, were to be instructed in 'the principles of the Church of England'.

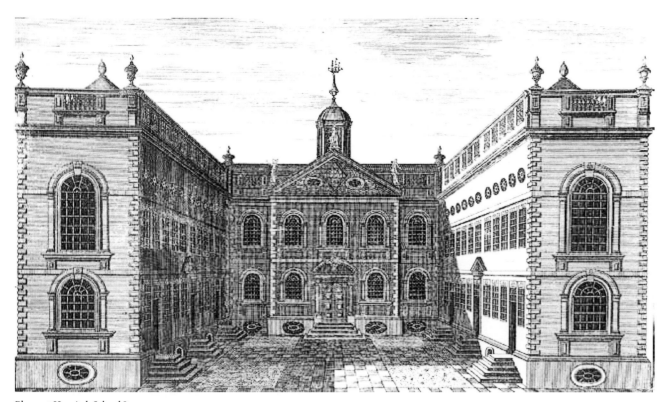

Bluecoat Hospital, School Lane

A third important building within the triangle was the Unitarian Chapel built in 1791 and located on Paradise Street at the corner of School Lane. A handsome, classical building with a lantern and dome surmounting a Corinthian pediment, it bore a strong superficial similarity to St Paul's Church. As has been mentioned the Unitarian denomination attracted many of the most distinguished of the Liverpool mercantile community, including William Roscoe and various members of the Rathbone family. This family and other members of this congregation played a very significant part in the Abolitionist Movement and in other philanthropic and intellectual activity within Liverpool and beyond. The chapel was in use until 1849, despite the declining character of the area. In that year, the congregation moved to a new church in Hope Street.

None of these buildings is included in the Brierley collection, though a drawing of St Peter's Church, listed in the acquisitions register of the Athenaeum, has been lost. The artist confines his efforts to the narrow streets that filled the rest of the triangle and each of the main lanes is depicted. The architecture shows that, in the main, the buildings date from the development of this area in the early decades of eighteenth century when the covering of the Pool Stream encouraged the town to spread into the new districts.

The picture of the Old House next to the Bluecoat Hospital shows the property which, in 1825 was occupied by Robert Fairclough as his cooperage. The building next door was the shop and residence of Joseph Garner, a tailor and draper. Both these occupants are recorded as being in the same properties in the Directory of 1829. On the left-hand margin of the picture are the railings which fronted the courtyard of the Bluecoat Hospital.

It is natural to suppose that the name School Lane is derived from the Bluecoat Hospital. This may be disputed as, prior to the building of the Bluecoat Hospital in 1716, the Liverpool Grammar School was located on a site almost opposite the new building, near where the present Athenaeum stands. Founded by John Crosse in 1515, it had moved from its original location in St Mary's Chapel on the waterfront when the building became too dilapidated for use. The date of the move from St Mary's is unknown but it is recorded that the preliminary meetings prior to the establishment of the Bluecoat Hospital were held in a room in the grammar school building. The Grammar School continued in School Lane until the death of the last Master, Mr Baines, in 1803. In its latter days, it seems to have worked in co-operation with its Bluecoat neighbours who used the upper floors of the building as a stocking factory, with the children from the Bluecoat providing the labour. This venture did not prove economic and production was turned over to pin making; again, the school children were set to work, a practice discontinued in 1802.

Further down School Lane, at the junction with Church Lane, as Brierley shows us, stood the public house of the *Lamb* kept in 1825 by Margaret Robinson, and marked by the barrel sign. In competition with Mrs Robinson was the *Old Ring of Bells*, located on the corner of School Lane and Peter's Lane, kept in 1825 by David McClive.

Manesty Lane takes its name from the wealthy merchant, ship owner and slave trader, Joseph Manesty, whose residence and counting house were in this street and who was the employer and patron of the young John Newton who later earned fame as a slaver, an abolitionist, a hymn writer and evangelical preacher.

Until the second half of the nineteenth century, a house stood at the corner of Manesty Lane and College Lane which dated to 1680 and was one of the earliest (if not the earliest) house to be erected by a Mr. Dansie on the east bank of the Pool. The house had a walled forecourt and imposing appearance. Later, it was the home of the distinguished physician, Dr Joseph Brandreth, an Ormskirk man who was one of the medical faculty of Liverpool which brought distinction to the town. Brandreth participated in many of the intellectual and cultural activities

Old House, School Lane, corner of Peters Lane, 1828

of the community, working at the Dispensary, the Infirmary and as physician to the Lunatic Asylum. He was twice President of the Liverpool Medical Institution, to which he contributed generously. The corner chosen by Brierley for his viewpoint is opposite the doctor's house and shows part of Hanover Street with a partial view down Manesty Lane. It has proved impossible to find either 'Burn's Cottage' or the tavern with its sign of a cock in any directory of the Brierley period.

Dr Joseph Brandreth 1746–1815
Amongst the most prominent of the Liverpool doctors, Joseph Brandreth
was born and first practised at Ormskirk before buying the practice of Dr
Matthew Dobson. Brandreth acted as a physician at both the Dispensary
– which he founded – and the Infirmary and was active in the Liverpool
Medical Institution. He developed the use of cold water in the treatment
of fever and published a pamphlet describing the practice.
[Athenaeum Proprietor No. 388]

The mercantile tradition of Manesty Lane seems to have been continued into Brierley's day. The street appears to have had no residents but one, and to have been filled with the counting houses, offices and premises of business men, agents, merchants, brokers, a vendor of feathers and provision wholesalers, though John Hargreaves and Joseph Barrow were both carriers and Francis Mason, who lived in the end house, was a teacher at the Charity School. The most unusual of the businesses in Manesty Lane was that of John Miller, a manufacturer of sulphur, Epsom salts and magnesia, he also traded as a dry salter or supplier of chemical products. This business of chemical and pharmaceutical supplier was in sharp contrast to that of his mercantile neighbours and may have been something of source of irritation to them as, by 1829, the building is described as only being an office.

Whitechapel and its adjacent streets - Button Street, Leigh Street, Derby Street, Cumberland Street

In the last fifty years, the area between Whitechapel and Victoria Street has been re-animated by the world prominence given to Mathew Street by the Beatles, an interest which has seen it develop a 'cafe quarter'. Its boutiques, chain store and the shadows of the Cavern Club bring a constant stream of visitors. The tangled warren of streets, alleys, narrow passageways and tall, old warehouses can confuse visitor and native alike. In a series of his smaller pictures, Brierley shows the area before its commercial development. In 1867, Victoria Street was driven through the district, radically altering the character of the area. Prior to this, Sir Thomas Street, Cumberland Street and Stanley Street ran through to Dale Street without a break. It was a district of small houses intermingled with shops, workshops and taverns. These had taken the place of important houses occupied by some of the most significant families of Liverpool, who had made their homes there as the new suburb developed in the early part of the eighteenth century, after the building of the dock.

On Whitechapel, between its junction with Lord Street and Button Street, was the workshop of Robert Barlow who, as the sign tells us, manufactured trunks and chests, items that must have had a considerable sale amongst Liverpool's sea-going population. This trade was well established in the Whitechapel area: Dorothy Hatch at 64 Whitechapel, and George Thompson in his workshop in Sir Thomas' Buildings were also makers of trunks. The building next to Barlow's is the ink factory and law stationery business of John Swinden. Button Street is not named for a commodity made there but after a Mr Button who, at his death in 1785, was the oldest burgess of Liverpool, being reputed to be at least one hundred years of age.

Old Houses, White Chapel, corner of Leigh Street, 1828

Almost opposite to these businesses was the entrance to Leigh Street, which led eastwards from Whitechapel. On the corner stood the King's Arms, kept by Peter Regan, while next door to the public house was the wine and spirit dealership of Anne Heighway. Beyond that, scarcely visible in the drawing, was the baker's shop of William Aldersey. Derby Street, named for the Earl of Derby, intersected the block between Cumberland Street and Stanley Street and reached a small square named Derby Square. This square was the site of a Baptist chapel built about 1750, erected for the use of a section of the Byrom Street congregation who had left that chapel after a disagreement. It remained as a place of worship until 1819 when the congregation moved to Great Crosshall Street. In addition to spiritual refreshment, Derby Square offered, as can be seen in the picture, the facilities of Langan's Spirit Vault.

Old House, White Chapel, corner of Derby Street, 1830

Old Houses, White Chapel, corner of Cumberland Street, 1828

Cumberland Street was named after Prince Ernest Augustus, the Duke of Cumberland and victor of Culloden. In the narrow street a small synagogue was the first Jewish place of worship in Liverpool. It was a simple square building facing south. The original congregation was of German origins, immigrants who, at first, seem to have been packmen and pedlars. They were later joined by merchants from Hamburg and London who spotted the commercial advantages of Liverpool, which they found a tolerant and welcoming place. The synagogue had a burial ground attached to it and during the development of the area in the mid-nineteenth century numerous fragments of human remains and grave stones with Hebrew inscriptions were found. The Jewish community moved to a new synagogue in Frederick Street in 1794, though the original building remained standing for some years. The fronts of several shops in Whitechapel are depicted. Easily identifiable is the book and print shop of John Davies at 81 Whitechapel, who, from the entries in the directories, seems to have specialised in antiquarian material. To the left of Davies' business was the shop of Catherine Anderton who dealt in flour and other similar products, while on the other side was Mary Tarbuck's fruiterer's shop.

St Andrew's Church, Renshaw Street, 1830

Located at the base of a triangle of roads formed by Renshaw, Bold and Heathfield Streets, this uninspired building – arguably the ugliest church in Liverpool – was erected in 1815 at a cost of £12,000, provided by John Gladstone (1764–1851). Architecturally, the building was dull and the style feeble. Its only interest was in the fact that, at a time when churches were designed as auditoria, St Andrew's had a chancel in the style of an earlier age. The area was one of increasing population, so much so that, in 1827, the building was extended. By the mid-century, the local population was declining and, by 1861, the graveyard was closed. In 1890, the site was bought by the Midland Railway and the church closed in December 1892. If the church had little artistic interest or historical significance, the career of its founder marked the impact of commerce and patronage on the development of Merseyside institutions.

The building of this church marked Gladstone's transition from Unitarianism – he had originally attended the Unitarian chapel in Renshaw Street where he was a friend of William Roscoe – to support for higher forms of Anglicanism.

John or Jack Gladstone was the eldest son of Thomas Gladstones, a corn chandler and Baltic merchant of Leith. After an apprenticeship, he worked in the family business before moving to Liverpool to work with Edgar Corrie, who suggested that the terminal 's' of his name was confusing. They traded in American tobacco and corn and it was on this that Gladstone based his fortune.

In 1801, John and his brothers started a new firm. Like many other Liverpool men, Gladstone became involved in the West Indian cotton and sugar trade and bought plantations, to run which he relied on slave labour. He never visited his plantations but accepted the word of his overseers that the slaves were well treated. On this he took his stance and found himself in vehement opposition to the abolitionists until 1807, when the slave trade was made illegal. In 1833, when total abolition of slavery in British territories was enacted, Gladstone sold his West Indian possessions and concentrated on trade with India, especially in sugar. John Gladstone became an extremely wealthy man and a leading figure in the social and political life of Liverpool. In politics he was originally a Whig Radical and supporter of Roscoe. He became a reforming Tory and managed George Canning's election for Liverpool between 1812 and 1820. He served as a Member of Parliament for various constituencies between 1820 and 1830. In the Corn Laws controversy, he opposed Peel, but despite this, he became a baronet in 1846.

In Liverpool, John Gladstone was one of the founder Proprietors of the Athenaeum (No. 172). His family lived in the house at No. 62 Rodney Street, probably built for him by John Whiteside Casson. In 1815, he purchased land in Litherland and built Seaforth House. In Liverpool, he founded both St Andrew's Church and an associated school for 150 boys and 130 girls. This building, dated 1818, can still be seen in Fleet Street. Gladstone's interest in education was also expressed in his support for the foundation of the Liverpool Collegiate School. He was responsible for the foundation of the Charitable Institution in Slater Street which provided free accommodation for local charities. In Litherland Marsh or, as it came to be called, Seaforth, Gladstone endowed the church of St Thomas in 1815. One of his last charitable benefactions in Liverpool was the funding of St Thomas' Church, Toxteth in 1840. In 1833, Gladstone left Merseyside and returned to Scotland and he purchased an estate at Fasque where he died 'a demanding and bitter man' in December 1851. It was his fourth son, William Ewart, who served four terms as Prime Minister.

John Gladstone 1764–1851

Born in Leith, John Gladstone [Athenaeum Proprietor No. 172] came to Liverpool in 1786 to set up in business as a corn factor. The business flourished and Gladstone's mercantile interests grew to include the importation of corn, tobacco and other commodities, ship owning and real estate. He became very wealthy, and in 1811, the family moved to the newly built Seaforth House at Litherland. A staunch and upright man, Gladstone was deeply interested in social reform and sponsored the establishment of schools and churches. W. E. Gladstone, four times Prime Minister, was his fourth son, born in Rodney Street in 1809.

A south view of St John's Church, 1830

By the middle of the eighteenth century, the area known as the Great Heath that lay to the east of the Pool Stream at the head of Dale Street had become a place of very mixed development. Much of the building on the land was made up of public works. It was the site of the Infirmary, the Seamen's Hospital, the Lunatic Asylum, and various almshouses. It was also an area where a number of markets were located. There was a general market on Commutation Row, on the land now occupied by the Wellington Column, a cattle market on Lime Street and the hay and fodder market filled the area to the west. Any remaining space was taken up with residential accommodation. There was no convenient church provision in this area so, when the Act of 1762 sanctioned the provision of two new churches in Liverpool, the Corporation decided to cater for the expansion in the Tithebarn Street area by the building of St Paul's (see page 117) and to select a site in the eastern side of the town for the second new church. The original intention had been to build on what is now Queen Square, then known as Patten's Garden and owned by Mr Samuel Shaw, but he declined to sell the land. The Corporation in its anxiety took a 999 year lease on land near the Haymarket to provide a church and perhaps, even more importantly, a burial place. The existing cemeteries were overcrowded and very often insanitary. Consequently, it was the graveyard with a small chapel that was provided, and building of the church did not commence until 1775. The cemetery at St John's was heavily used, and burials included the interment of 240 French prisoners of war who had died in captivity.

The architect of the new church was to be Timothy Lightoller. His design for St Paul's had been very much in the style of the English Baroque – there is some suggestion that he was trying to emulate its London namesake – but now he adopted the newly fashionable 'Gothick'. The design was weak and uninteresting, the style a vague imitation of the Perpendicular, the nave with a clerestory and pinnacle parapet – though surviving photographs show that either this feature was altered to a more Jacobean style or that Brierley's depiction is inaccurate. A new development was the small chancel and a tower of unexciting proportions. Building began in 1775 and the completed church was consecrated in 1783.

The fortunes of the church were not improved when much of the surrounding land was cleared to provide the site for the new St George's Hall, construction of which began in 1840 and was not completed until 1854. This new building was in sharp contrast to the feeble Gothic of the church thrust against its western side which obscured the view of the west front of the Hall. The church survived until 1898 when it was no longer of any significant use. In that year, it was closed and demolition followed shortly after. The burial ground was cleared and landscaped to become a raised terrace and garden which was soon being used as a place to display the statues of the great and the good of the City.

In this drawing, Brierley seems to have encountered more than his usual difficulties of perspective and proportion. To the left of St John's, the belfry of St Stephen's church in Byrom Street can be seen while to the right Islington Mill protrudes above the buildings. The traffic in Old Haymarket includes a minuscule stage coach with outside passengers. The ubiquitous gentleman with the umbrella strolls up the hill!

A view of St Matthew's Church, Key Street, 1830

The origins of St Matthew's Church lay in the early eighteenth century. In 1706, a licence was granted to the English Presbyterian Non-conformists of Liverpool to build a chapel in what was then a new street running from Tithebarn Street towards the Town Fields. The Toleration Act of 1689 gave Non-conformist groups permission to establish licensed places of public worship, and to appoint their own ministers and teachers. The first minister of Key Street chapel was Christopher Basnett, whose name is commemorated in Basnett Street. Non-conformists still remained excluded from public office, though occasional attendance at Anglican worship and the taking of the sacraments did allow them to hold civic posts.

In 1791, the Key Street Chapel became redundant when a new chapel was erected in Paradise Street, a gracious, domed, classical building. The redundant chapel was purchased by the Church of England and consecrated as St Matthew's Church. The building drawn by Brierley has the simplicity and Spartan functionality of a Meeting House. The moderate decorative flourish of the bell cote and urn over the side entrance was probably added by the Established Church.

Twenty years after Brierley's portrayal, the church found itself threatened by railway developments. In 1848, Tithebarn Street Station had been built to replace the earlier Great Howard Street Station as the terminus for three railways, the Liverpool, Crosby and Southport Railway, the Liverpool and Bury Company, and the Liverpool, Ormskirk and Preston line. In 1850, the station was extended, enlarged and renamed as Exchange Station to become the terminus of the Lancashire and Yorkshire Railway. In order to carry out the station project, the demolition of St Matthew's was proposed. However, the protests of the then vicar, Dr Hilcoat, and his demand that the churchyard be purchased at the price of commercial land, sparked a long case in Queen's Bench. Hilcoat won his case and received substantial compensation. This judgement set a precedent that established the law in these cases for many years. As part of the compensation agreement, the Lancashire and Yorkshire Railway Company purchased a former Scottish Church on Scotland Road which became the new St Matthew's.

It is impossible now to determine the precise site of the church in Key Street, the whole area having been completely demolished and covered by railway property. This, in turn, has now disappeared and the car park off Pall Mall covers the site of St Matthew's.

A south east view of St Michael's Church, 1830

On 6 February 1793, a petition to the Liverpool Corporation pointed out that the 'The inhabitants … are now become so very numerous that the present churches … are by no means able to contain the inhabitants … desirous to worship according to the rights and ceremonies of the Church of England'. The petitioners asked the Corporation to build a new church and offered, at their own expense, to provide another. Nothing further seems to have followed; presumably the outbreak of the French war in that year and the resulting decline in trade diverted their minds.

On 5 February 1800, the Corporation received a letter from the Vestry Clerk, Edward Blackstock, to the effect that the scheme had been revived. A proposal was made that a suitable site would be the ground between St James' Street and Great George Street, formerly part of the pleasure grounds of Mr Moses Benson's house in Duke Street (see page 101). Approval was given by the Corporation and work began in 1816 on a plan prepared by the younger John Foster. In this building Foster does not attempt the same scholarly rendition of a Greek design that he had used in the Blind School Chapel (see page 87) but harks back to English Baroque, though some of the detail shows evidence of his classical studies, notably in the Corinthian columns that frame the portico. Architectural critics applauded the design of the portico because its depth helped create a mysterious and shaded entrance. One of the most eye-catching features of the church was the steeple, 201 feet high, though, after a lightning strike in 1841, the upper part was demolished and never rebuilt.

By 1823, when the Parish Vestry had spent £34,500 on the building, they became concerned that the additional £10,000 estimated to be necessary to complete the building was not available. On 30 January 1823 the Vestry laid the situation before the Council which, at this time, was extremely wealthy, had little to spend its money on and could sometimes be persuaded to act 'as the good fairy in the nursery tale'. To the relief of those involved, the Corporation agreed to make good the shortfall and spent another £10,267 10s. 6d. on completing the work in 1825. The church, heavily damaged by bombing during the Second World War, was later demolished and a new building erected on the same site.

For this painting Brierley, has chosen a viewpoint in Cornwallis Street, looking north west. Behind the church, in its railed enclosure, the houses in Grenville Street can be seen, while at the western end of the church is Upper Pitt Street and Frederick Street. These houses date from the development of the area south of Duke Street, which occurred in the first decade of the nineteenth century. In this drawing, Brierley has attempted to animate the scene by introducing six figures into the view. Though five of them are fashionably dressed, including the stout gentleman with his umbrella, we also see a woman with a basket of fruit or flowers on her head, peddling her wares. On the corner of the street can be seen a street lamp, a rare sight in Brierley's world. In earlier times, oil lamps were used to illuminate the streets. In 1718, Mr Halsall had undertaken the care and maintenance of street lanterns at a charge of 10s. per lamp per annum. The first gas lights were installed at the Town Hall in 1816 as a special demonstration and it was in 1818 that a Gaslight Company and the use of gas for street lighting were approved. The blinding benefits of the introduction of gas lights can be imagined.

A view of St Paul's Church, 1830

'For some reason or another, this building seems always to have been under a cloud,' wrote James Picton when describing this rather opulent and magnificent building, designed by Timothy Lightoller and built at the expense of the Corporation as part of the increased provision of churches in the town. A Council resolution of 7 November 1753 authorised the venture but it was not until 1760 that the project went ahead, with completion in 1769. Lightoller was frequently used as an architect and master mason by the Corporation for the design of public buildings, including the lighthouse at Leasowe and St John's Church. The site selected for St Paul's was in a newly developing residential area located north and west of Tithebarn Street, unglamorously known as 'Dog Field'. The building of the church was accompanied by the erection of houses around the square and the new, adjoining streets.

Though the church was impressive, it failed to attract a congregation of any size, perhaps because of the appalling acoustics. The surrounding area became the centre of the resident Welsh population and services in that language were held in St Paul's. Even the first incumbent was slightly unusual. He was the Reverend John Harrison who, from 1752 until 1763, had been the Minister of the Dissenting Chapel in Benn's Gardens but who had conformed to the Established Church.

In 1777, a great bell was mounted in the dome of St Paul's, the joiner's work being done by John Foster, the founder of the family's fortune and grandfather of John Foster the Younger. In 1802, moves were made to have an organ installed and, in 1825, St Paul's had the clock placed in the cupola of the dome and, in a revolutionary move, this was illuminated with gas, apparently the first illuminated clock in Liverpool. Perhaps the necessary apparatus for the gas supply was enclosed in the strange louvered box shown by Brierley over the portico. The church continued in use as the area around it declined to one of warehousing, commercial premises and, after 1848, the railway and sidings of the Tithebarn (later Exchange) Station.

In 1817, St Paul's Square became the focus of a strange and sensational story. A seventeen year old woman, Miss McAvoy, suffered from partial paralysis and was considered to be totally without sight. Suddenly, she developed an ability to read print and distinguish colours by touch alone. She could even perform this feat with her eyes blindfolded. The story was widely reported and supported by a pamphlet written by Dr Renwick, a prominent Liverpool medical man. Crowds flocked to St Paul's Square to see her perform the miracle. Contemporary reports stress that she could read the smallest print and distinguish delicate shades of colour but that she made no attempt to profit from her powers.

With use and attention her abilities increased and soon, with nothing more than her finger tips on a window, she could describe people in the churchyard and even detail their clothes. She claimed that in order to work there had to be nothing between her eyes and her hands because it was essential that her breath should be uninterrupted. Mr Egerton Smith then devised a mask which covered her eyes but in no way hindered her breath and offered twenty guineas, a sum doubled by another sceptic, for her to perform her miracle whilst wearing the mask. After some discussion, she declined to take the challenge and lost all credibility, dying some two years later.

St Paul's closed for worship in 1901 and the site was bought by the Lancashire & Yorkshire Railway Company for planned expansion of the station. This did not happen, and, instead the celebrated Liverpool Stadium, scene of memorable boxing events, was built on the spot.

A view of St Stephen's Church, Byrom Street, 1830

James Brierley included two almost identical views of this church in his portfolio for the Athenaeum. Careful examination shows that there are slight variations in the viewpoint, with the church building filling more of the space on the paper in one view. His handling of the sky and clouds differs between the two versions and the beloved smoke from the chimneys – so much a feature of the artist's view of Liverpool – is not the same.

St Stephen's stood on Byrom Street at the foot of Shaw's Brow or William Brown Street, as it is known today, the actual location of the church being under the car park and flyover of Churchill Way.

Like St Matthew's in Key Street (see page 113), St Stephen's was an example of the ecclesiastical recycling that was evident in the frenetic expansion of churches within Liverpool. In the century ending in 1851, the number of Anglican churches in Liverpool increased from 6 to 51. During the same period, the provision for Non-conformists and Roman Catholic places of worship grew proportionately.

The original building of St Stephen's was a Baptist chapel, established in 1722 by the followers of Dr Fabius, a medical man, and was the first purpose-built place of worship for that denomination in Liverpool. It has been suggested that Fabius was of German origin and that his actual name was Bean, but the Latin translation of the name might have been thought to have greater gravitas. It is an interesting reflection on the religious attitudes of the period that a devout Roman Catholic, such as the diarist Nicholas Blundell, made use of Fabius' services when his wife was pregnant. Bean died in 1718 so the chapel must have been founded posthumously.

Fabius' congregation was the earliest recorded group of Baptists in Liverpool (1700) and is first mentioned meeting at his house on the corner of Everton Road and Brunswick Road. In 1710, the Corporation noted that a house at the foot of James Street was used for a meeting of Protestant Dissenters, led by the doctor. As their numbers grew, a barn in Townsend Lane became their meeting place (1722). They seem to have drawn their inspiration from the congregation of a chapel at Hill Cliffe, near Warrington. On the opening of the Byrom Street Chapel members of the congregation complained that it was too far outside the town. Despite this, the Liverpool community of Baptists increased, perhaps through the ministries of distinguished preachers. From 1741, the Minister was the Reverend Mr Johnson, a descendant of the celebrated Sir Thomas Johnson, a man of great significance in the early development of the town. Johnson was followed in 1772 by the Reverend Samuel Medley, or Bo'sun Medley. In his youth he had served as Midshipman and Master's Mate in the Royal Navy until wounded at the Battle of Lagos in 1759. He became a schoolmaster and then a Baptist minister. Medley was especially effective as a preacher amongst the seafaring community and the congregation grew until in 1773 the chapel was enlarged and in, 1789, moved to a new building in Gerrard Street. This remained the main chapel of the Baptists until the community was split by a doctrinal dispute.

The old chapel was sold to the Church of England and consecrated as St Stephen's by the Bishop of Chester in 1792. It continued in being until the late 1860s when the building was abandoned and replaced by a new church.

A view of St Thomas' Church, 1830

In the middle years of the eighteenth century, Liverpool began to expand beyond its original boundaries and much of this early growth occurred in the area to the south east of the head of the Pool along the axes of growth of the new and fashionable Duke Street – named for the Duke of Cumberland – and Park Road, the original track to Toxteth. Among the new streets and squares was Lydia Ann Street where, at one time, the Brierley family was resident at No. 7.

Some family members were connected with St Thomas' Church, as their marriages and baptisms are recorded there.

A resolution of the Vestry on 28 January 1747 and presented in January 1748 to the Corporation was intended to provide ecclesiastical provision for the new areas. 'Several well-disposed persons who had lately subscribed the sume [sic] of two thousand three hundred pounds and upwards towards the building of a new church or chapel in Mr Okills' ground near Park Lane'. The advowson of this new church was to be vested in the Corporation. This procedure was agreed and the Corporation undertook the expense of obtaining the Act of Parliament.

In January 1748 a meeting was held between some of the Commissioners of the church and Mr Okill concerning the piece of land, intended to be bought for the burial ground. In the March of that year a delegation of the Corporation was sent 'to Quarry Hill where the land had been feyed [that is, vegetation and topsoil removed] to allow the contractors for the church to take it for the use of the church and to fix what price they shall pay'. Quarry Hill, later known as St James' Mount, was an ideal source of building stone given its proximity to the site of the church and the relatively easy access to Duke Street.

Old Houses, Moor Street, corner of Fenwick Street 1828.

The Directories of 1825 and 1829 confirm the decline of the resident population. Apart from the obligatory public houses, one kept by Robert Gardener, who was also a Master Mariner, a variety of houses and shops filled the street. William Griffiths, a mariner, lived in the corner house and at No. 15 Mrs E. Pattern kept a boarding house. There was a fishmonger and a fruiterer, a corn merchant and a boat owner (who in 1829 is recorded as a shipbuilder), a basket maker and a plasterer, a hair dresser and a surgeon, a ham curer and provision merchant and a manufacturer of chains 'on an improved principal'. William Sidney ran a public bake house, which probably did well in view of the regulation that the galley fires of ships must be extinguished while the vessel was in dock.

Old houses, New Key, 1828

A great deal of the early history of the extent, operation and even location of the original port of Liverpool is largely unknown but we know a great deal about the genesis of New Quay or Key from the notes of Sir Edward Moore, who wrote in his rental

… Remember to build a wall all along the bank side till you come to the Town Field; otherwise in time, I am afraid, the sea will wear away the whole bank … it is so much worn away with the sea … When you make the wall, it need not be above two yards high and two feet thick, then fill the earth to the back of it: – this wall will cost about £90 at the most. If it be possible, get warehouses or dwelling houses built all along the wall and make a street to go up in the very middle of it through to the north of the Old Hall. [*Liverpool in the Time of Charles II* ed. W. F. Irvine Liverpool 1899.]

Shortly after the above passage was written, the wall was built and 'New Quay' created. The town records show that, by 1672, work had begun and, on 18 September 1676, there was some discussion between Moore and the Mayor and Corporation concerning the wall and the development of the area. The outcome of these talks seems to have been that Moore agreed to transfer ownership of the quay to the Corporation. On Chadwick's map of Liverpool, dated 1725, 'New Key' is clearly marked and is shown as fully built-up along its inland side. Eyes' map of 1765 shows some development of embayments in the wall, presumably to provide shelter for small boats, and also marks a sloping earth bank behind the buildings up to the rear of the houses in Lancelot's Hey. The intention, expressed by Edward Moore, of linking the quay to Old Hall Street had been accomplished by the building of Union Street.

The two buildings in the centre of the drawing can be dated stylistically to the period of the building of the wall, though it is apparent that the four storey tower on the premises occupied by J. Cross is a later addition. The Baines' Directory of 1825 lists J. Cross as a pump and block maker (these would have been the pulley blocks used in the rigging of ships) at No. 14. The premises were shared with four other concerns: T. Croston & Co., who were ropers, ship chandlers, painters, plumbers and glaziers; Josiah Dancer, an optician, who was probably more concerned with making optical and navigational instruments; Humble & Hurry and R. & J. Russell, who were boat and ship builders and also makers of anchors and chains. The building, with the conspicuous sign board, is the shop of Patrick Connor, a dealer in marine stores.

There was a definite nautical air pervading the atmosphere of New Quay. In all, there are twenty-four addresses listed in the 1825 Directory, of which eight are places of refreshment with names like The Packet, The Dolphin and The Swan. The Crown and Castle and The Prince of Wales' Feather' were kept by Hugh Hughes and Ann Hughes respectively. There were six merchants' offices, three of whom were also ship owners. In addition, there were several of other marine traders: ship chandlers, ropemakers, anchor and chain smiths, boat and shipbuilders.

By 1829 many of these businesses had closed or removed to new addresses. The demand for warehouse space for the new Prince's Dock (opened 1830) possibly precipitated this exodus. Later paintings from the late nineteenth century show New Quay lined with warehouses.

A view of buildings, Nova Scotia, 1830

The construction of George's Dock began in 1762 and was the first built parallel to the river and so required a sea wall. The dock was entered either at its northern end or by a channel that connected it to the Dry Dock of 1715. Spoil from the excavation was dumped on the seaward side of the wall to create an embankment. When the later Manchester and Chester docks were built, the bank was extended and broadened. As the sea wall was pushed further and further out from the old shoreline it created more land on which the larger buildings were constructed. It is not always realised that much of the famous Liverpool waterfront – including the sites of the Three Graces – are on reclaimed land well beyond the ancient tide line.

The name Nova Scotia was probably an ironic reference to the remote location, its separation by water and its bleak aspect. Though originally a narrow strip of land, subsequent dock work and further reclamation more than doubled the width and it became an area where 'amongst the offices of the Dublin and Isle of Man Packets and the Manchester flats were tar warehouses, coal merchants, blockmakers, public houses and dwellings of river pilots and boatmen' [Liverpool's Historic Waterfront, N. Ritchie-Noakes HMSO London 1984].

By 1830 the buildings on Nova Scotia comprised two blocks in commercial occupation and one terrace of housing, though evidence from recent excavations shows that several of these houses contained the workshops of craftsmen, intermingled with their living accommodation. In 1824, according

to Baines' Directory, apart from the house of William Jones, Master of the Dry Dock, the rest of the thirteen houses were licensed premises, which included the Ship, New Ferry Boat, Grapes, Ship and Punch Bowl, Bull's Head and the Tranmere Boat House. James Slater, landlord of an unnamed ale house was also a river pilot. Excavation in the period 2006–09 has shown that these houses were single room dwellings, of two or more storeys and constructed of hand-made brick and occasional pieces of yellow sandstone.

The warehouse shown on the drawing of Nova Scotia is a good illustration of the design and construction of many of the early warehouses before the regulation of their materials and constructional techniques was introduced by the local Building Acts passed between 1825 and 1843. These regulations, largely inspired by the destruction of the Goree warehouses in 1833, were concerned with minimising the fire risk and reducing the opportunities for pilfering. The early structures, brick built, with flat frontages on the roadway, were built to a considerable height in order to create the maximum storage space on as small a ground area as possible. A pitched roof was supported on substantial timber trusses. The frontage usually had a central bay which was filled with a series of loading doors and was surmounted by a hoist beam. In some cases this was operated by man-powered windlasses, contained in the 'jigger loft'. Access to the warehouse was through narrow street doors located at the foot of each stack, made deliberately small to make pilfering difficult. This door opened on to a spiral wooden staircase, often with a central newel. An indication of the position of the stairs can be gained through the presence of small, round windows, often filled with an iron grille, again as an anti-theft device. Occasionally, as in the case of the central block in the drawing of Nova Scotia, an external man-operated crane was placed outside the building for handling goods on and off the horse-drawn wagons. Most of these features can be discerned in the buildings shown in Brierley's pictures of the dockside area. The warehouse on Nova Scotia accommodated a firm of sailmakers, Blackburne's the salt merchants, a corn and hop dealer, R. & T. Woodward and Roswell, lead merchants. [For descriptions of warehouse construction see Storehouses of Empire: Liverpool's Historic Warehouses, Giles & Hawkins, English Heritage, 2004.]

The two packet offices shown are a clear reminder of the important part played by coastal shipping before the development of rail and road transport. The directories of the early nineteenth century have elaborate lists of coastal and packet boats whose services were available. No fewer than 114 routes were listed to destinations ranging from Lisbon to New York. The first block of buildings comprised three public houses. No. 1 was a public house of which John Bolton was the landlord. Next door were the premises of Shanklin, Manley & Co. who were the agents at the Chester Canal Office. At No. 5 Irwell Street were the offices of the 'New Mersey and Irwell Navigation Company', whose boats plied to Warrington and then on to Manchester. The trade on this Navigation was in the hands of two companies and adjacent to No. 5 William Guyton acted as agent for the 'Old River Company', a situation likely to provoke violent rivalry. It seems probable that this is the building visible in the picture and extending on to Mann Island.

Both Mann Island and Nova Scotia have vanished entirely, though the name of Mann Island is still used as a street name. Recent archaeological investigation has done much to confirm the accuracy of Brierley's portrayal of this area and the validity of Ritchie-Noakes' description. Today, little remains visible on the surface, though the hydraulic tower which operated the gates between Canning and George's Dock still stands, and a few yards of the passage can still be discerned at the north-east corner of Canning Dock. A portion of the wall of George's Dock can be seen by visitors to the basement of the Cunard Building. The preparatory work on the site of the Museum of Liverpool Life uncovered extraordinarily well-preserved remains of the Manchester Dock which was used in 1928 as a dumping ground for spoil from the Mersey Tunnel. It was from this dock that the Manchester and Runcorn packets, whose warehouse and booking office were on Nova Scotia, made their crossings.

This drawing of the Mulberry or Marlbrough. the first ship to enter the Dock, was drawn by Bryan Blundell, its master and owner in his Journal now held in the Lancashire Archives'

The series of drawings by James Brierley of the buildings surrounding the Old Dock carry great historical significance. The building of the dock was one of the great landmarks in the history of Liverpool. All subsequent development of the port was based on this construction and its successors.

When Brierley made his drawings he was recording the demise of the dock which had become redundant. Plans were well advanced for the basin to be filled in and for the new and very much enlarged Custom House to be raised on its site. The new building, with its massive, classical solidity was probably the most successful design of John Foster the Younger. The building was destroyed by enemy action during the Second World War and replaced by tower blocks, thus obliterating, for more than fifty years, the last reminder of this significant step in Liverpool's maritime origins. Only in the new century has the Old Dock re-emerged as a result of the Liverpool One development and is once more on view.

The early development of the port of Liverpool was hampered by the geographic and navigational problems of the Mersey as a harbour. Strong tides, a wide tidal range and the direction of the prevailing winds caused problems for sailing ships. Cargo was discharged either in more sheltered parts of the estuary or vessels were beached to allow cargo handling. The expense and difficulties of working ships in this way had led to attempts to improve the port facilities but these had largely proved nugatory.

In the last decades of the seventeenth century there were discussions about the possibility of enhancing the port's provision. Added impetus was given by the town's new charter of 1695 which put civic control in the hands of the mercantile elite, always anxious to develop trade. Added immediacy was given to the plans when, in 1703, the shipping in the river was devastated by the Great Hurricane.

Various proposals were made for the enhancement of the port facilities and the concept of a new, wet dock in which ships could ride at the same level at any stage of the tide was an innovative idea. Earlier docks of this sort had been built in other ports, including London and Portsmouth, but were not intended for cargo handling. The plan to build a facility where ships could load or unload while floating at the level of the wharf and be safely moored, regardless of weather and tidal conditions, was revolutionary.

On 3 November 1708, the town's Members of Parliament, Sir Thomas Johnson, a Liverpool tobacco merchant, and Richard Norris, a merchant, were commissioned by the Corporation to petition for a Bill to authorise the construction of a dock. George Sorocold, an engineer, possibly with industrial hydraulic experience at Derby, was invited to prepare a plan, in which he was assisted by Henry Huss of Derbyshire. The two made a survey in April 1709. Their plan was to isolate the Pool from the river by watertight lock gates so that the remains of the Pool could be dredged and canalised. This proposal was accepted but for some reason never put into effect. Sorocold left Liverpool for work elsewhere.

He was replaced by Thomas Steers (c.1670–1750), a former soldier in the army of William III, who had designed some salt works on the River Boyne and studied Dutch hydraulic engineering during his military service. His suggested plan for Liverpool was bolder and even more innovative than its predecessor. Steers proposed that the stream which fed the Pool should be culverted and that a stone tank should be constructed with lock gates at its seaward end. The dock would join the Mersey by a short entrance passage. On this channel, a half-tide basin, with a graving dock for ship repairs, was to be built. It was suggested that a wooden pier or jetty projecting into the river would allow ships entering or leaving the dock to moor whilst waiting for favourable conditions. The portion of the Pool not enclosed within the dock would be filled in and on the reclaimed land the Corporation would erect warehouses and other buildings, the rent from which would help to meet the building costs of the dock.

By 1710 the scheme was ready to be presented to Parliament in order to obtain an authorising Act. The matter was thus explained '…so difficult and dangerous …[was the entrance to the port] that great numbers of strangers, and others, have frequently lost their lives, with ships and goods, for want of proper landing, buoys and other directions into it; and more especially, for want of a convenient wet dock or basin'. To defray the constructional costs, the Act authorised an additional charge to be placed on all shipping using the Mersey. This proposal aroused organised opposition from the cheese merchants of Cheshire, whose coasters, which used harbours on the Cheshire side of the river, would have to pay dues towards the cost of a dock they would never use. Their protests were over-ruled and the Corporation was authorised to raise £6,000, a totally inadequate sum for the project. Thomas Steers was appointed Dock Engineer in 1710 and work began.

We know little about the actual construction but recent excavation shows that the dock was roughly rectangular and enclosed three and a half acres. It was brick-lined with a stone coping and its lower portions were dug into the bedrock.

By 31 August 1715 the dock, if not fully completed, was opened for use. The local diarist Nicholas Blundell was there. 'I went to Leverpoole and saw the Mulberry, the Batchelor & the Robert all in the Dock, they came in this morning & were the first ships as ever went into it; the Mulberry was first … at the lower end of Red Cross Street I saw an ox roasting.' By a remarkable historical chance a coloured drawing by Bryan Blundell, master and owner of the Mulberry, with which he illustrated his journal, survives. It is now kept in the Lancashire Archives [LRO DDBb].

The new dock proved immensely successful. Plans were drawn up for the building of additional docks utilising what had been learned from the pioneering experience of what was soon known as 'The Old Dock'. However, the cost of building the Old Dock far exceeded the original estimate of £6,000 and, at times, the Corporation was at shifts to raise the necessary cash, being forced to borrow against projected dock dues. The final cost of building was £11,000: a second Act of Parliament was obtained in 1717 in order to raise this sum.

By the 1820s the quays of the Old Dock were too narrow, the wharfs were too small and much of the interior space, intended for the laying-up of ships, was now redundant. Additionally, the amount of sewage in the dock was becoming increasingly unpleasant and, it was suggested, dangerous to health. Initial Parliamentary consent to the closure and reclamation of the Old Dock came in an Act of 1809 but, apart from authorising that the work should be done, little effort was made to take it in hand. In September 1809, the concept of a new Custom House and a new street from Pool Lane to Mersey Street was approved but no action was taken (This street was, in fact, never built).

The plan for the reclamation of the ground and the building of the Custom House was revived in 1823. In 1825, the Dock Committee was pressed to start work and the decision to build the new Custom House was supported as '... Conducive to the comfort and convenience of the merchants and other inhabitants of the town'. However, this was not the opinion of the Liverpool Ship Owners' Association who petitioned the Council against the project, but, by December 1826, John Foster's plans were approved, and work began on infilling the basin.

The foundation stone of the new Custom House was laid on 12 August 1828; the work would have been going on as Brierley made his drawings, so we can see these illustrations as the last knell of the area which had spawned so much of Liverpool's growth.

The Old Dock led the way and its outstanding success, which proved too much for its resources, soon led to the expansion of the dock system, first at Salthouse Dock in 1758, then at George's Dock in 1771, King's Dock 1789 and the Queen's Dock of 1796. These, with various smaller basins, provided the nucleus for the great expansion of the dock system by Foster and Hartley in the years after 1800.

The Old Dock with St. Thomas' Church. Based on a drawing by Peter Perez Burdett this later watercolour shows the Old Dock in its heyday. To the left stands the Custom House, flying a pre Union of 1800 flag. St Thomas, its spire still intact dominated the background. The advantage of the dock in cargo handling is clearly evident as the carts are able to go alongside the ships and take on their loads directly. [Picture from the Athenaeum collection]

Buildings, North Side Old Dock, 1830

In this series of drawings, it is unsafe to assume that they form a complete, interlocking panorama of the dock sides. It does seem that there are gaps between the sections depicted.

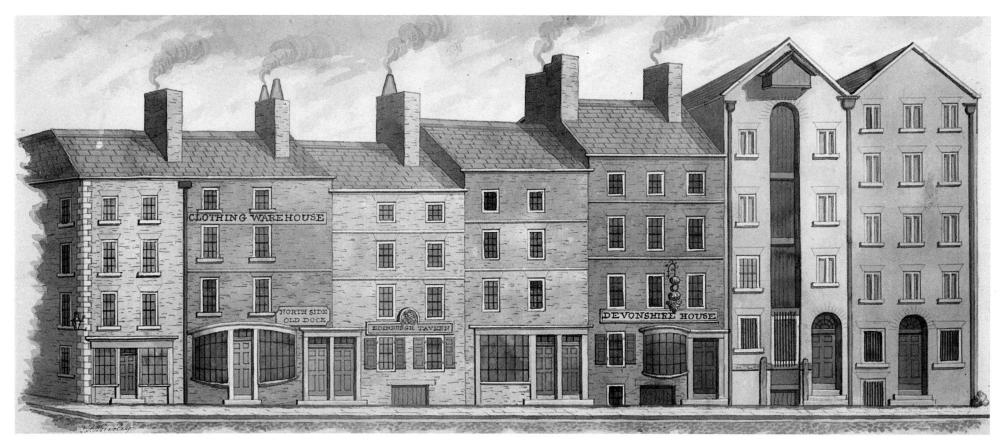

Picture 1

This shows the buildings from the eastern corner of Strand Street to Crooked Lane and comprises Nos 6 to 11. The building to the left-hand side is the Caledonian Tavern, kept by Michael Heaney, while next door the premises marked 'Clothing Warehouse' were those of Nathan Samuel, who was also a navy agent, that is, one who managed naval officers' pay or prize money. The Edinburgh Tavern was run by Ellen Jones, while the neighbouring shop was the place of business of John Fearn, a shopkeeper, presumably a general dealer, as he does not appear in any specialised list. The public house at No. 10, here named the Devonshire House was, in 1825, the Bristol Tavern of which the landlady was Margaret Slater. The twin warehouse type of building at the end of the block contained the offices and stores of two, apparently linked businesses Gills & Thompson and W. & J. Thompson, who were both merchants.

Picture 2

In this picture, Brierley continues his panorama of Old Dock; in this section he covers the frontage from Crooked Alley to Pool Lane. Something of a mystery surrounds No. 13 on the corner of Crooked Lane. Though clearly shown here as the Montrose Tavern, the directories of both 1825 and 1829 confirm it as the shop of Samuel Hargreaves, tailor, slop dealer and draper. Another slop dealer, Eliza Nugent, had the shop next door and at No. 15 John Madrell conducted his business as a boot and shoe maker. The landlord of the Clarence Tavern was Dominic Dale. On the opposite corner of Litherland Alley, William Kermode, a jack-of-all-trades, worked as a plumber, glazier, painter, grocer and flour dealer in premises shared with the slop dealer, Patrick Murray. The industrial building on the corner of Pool Lane appears to be two separate premises but the twin doors led to different stacks of the warehouse as a security measure. The building was occupied by T. & H. Lacon, iron founders.

Picture 3

As the title of this drawing indicates, it completes the panorama of the Old Dock, North Side with its depiction of the buildings between Pool Lane and South John Street. The building with the projecting sign is the sail loft of Samuel Lennox. To the right of his works are the stores of John Sinclair a provision merchant and ship owner. Other brokers, merchants and agents fill the other premises shown here. A slight oddity is the shop of Joseph Robinson who was not only an ironmonger but also an agent for Slater's patent steam stoves. Such a stove had been installed in the Brownlow Hill workhouse, with very satisfactory results.

Buildings, South Side Old Dock

Picture 1

This shows the range of buildings between Frederick Street on the left and the entrance to Rock Lane. The flat-fronted building on the left was the Puncheon kept by John Taylor. The building next door, which retains the Dutch gables of the warehouses built around the Old Dock in its very early days, was the depository for Davenport and Co., earthenware and glass makers of Longport in Staffordshire. Their presence is a reminder of the way in which the water-borne transport of the canals aided the development of national and international trade in fragile commodities. The premises on the next corner of Rock Lane were occupied by Hannah Pryce, but her name and details are omitted from the directory for both 1825 and 1829. The public house is the Commercial Tavern, whose landlord was William Shaw, while next door the building with the shutters, was also an inn, the Hope and Anchor, kept by Jane Parry.

Picture 2

The panorama continues with this drawing which shows the entrance to Mersey Street and the buildings which extended westward. Behind the buildings in the centre, an alleyway led to a yard with industrial buildings. The building with shutters on the corner of Mersey Street is the public house of Joseph Hatton and on the opposite corner the Whitehaven Tavern was kept by John Proctor.

Picture 3

In 1825, the Crown and Thistle, clearly identifiable here, was kept by William Long and the adjoining business had been a wine and porter dealers, run by Isaac Malker, while the upper floor housed the offices of John Rideing. Rideing is listed as a commission agent, merchant and ship owner. It may be that his vessels were engaged in fishing, as he also owned a herring house in Gradwell Street where fish was cured and smoked. However, it is clearly apparent from the sign that, by 1830, a barber had taken his place on the ground floor. The warehouse buildings were the premises of Clint and Company, bakers of ships' bread.

Buildings, Darwin Street, corner of South Side Old Dock, 1830

Once more in this illustration, Brierley is recording buildings and streets which were under threat. Darwin Street was a very short passageway which ran from the south east corner of the south wall of the Old Dock through to the northern quay of Salthouse Dock. The street was built after the opening of the Old Dock in 1715 and the construction of Salthouse Dock in its original form. This new dock was begun in 1738 to the design of Thomas Steers, but its construction was very slow, largely due to the fact that much of the proposed area was filled with leased ship-yards and other maritime businesses. Consequently, the dock was not operational until 1753. Darwin Street was located on the knuckle of the pier that separated Salthouse Dock from the entrance passage of the Old Dock.

The lane was more than adequately supplied with public houses – no fewer than four of the six addresses given in the 1825 Directory fall into this category. Most of them were simply sailors' ale houses but the one shown in the picture – Woodcock's – represents a more considerable enterprise. The Directory for 1821 lists only two people of the name Woodcock, one of whom is John, a victualler at 82 West End, Old Dock. Baines' Directory of 1825 repeats this entry. By 1829 Woodcock is listed as a Victualler at 5, East Side, Salthouse Dock and also at the same address is recorded as a wholesale and retail wine and spirit dealer. This directory also has an entry for a John Woodcock as a wine and spirit merchant at an address in Upper Pitt Street.

The Baines' Directory of 1825 lists six occupied buildings in Darwin Street. As we have seen, four of these are public houses. The others are the ships' chandlery business of George Clare and the house of P. McMillan, a sailor. The ale houses listed include a nameless public house run by William Roberts, the Rose and Thistle of Rylands Sale, who also had a subsidiary business as a ship broker. The others were the Highland Man, kept by Hugh Griffiths and the Yarmouth Arms of Martha Ball. There is no mention of the Bristol and Cardigan Bay tavern shown in the illustration.

Most of Brierley's drawing is taken up by a large warehouse clearly labelled Fisher Robinson. In fact, this building was not considered to be in Darwin Street but is listed in the directories as 72, Old Dock South Side. The accommodation was shared by the vaults of Fisher and Robinson, wine merchants, and another partnership, Fisher, Robinson and Martin who traded as provision dealers. This dual use may explain the additional warehouse doors and hoists on the Darwin Street side of the building.

A view of the old public house, Chapel Street, 1820

The traditional relationship between the church building and the local public house is clearly manifest in this picture. The conjunction was necessary in rural areas where the congregation had made a journey to arrive for worship and needed stabling and refreshment. However, the proximity could seduce people from their religious duties; one of the responsibilities of the Wardens of the church was to ensure that the public houses were shut during the time of divine service.

The burial grounds for Liverpool and St Nicholas' Chapel were established in 1361 by the Bishop of Lichfield and Coventry and were accessed by steps to the Strand, while a second entrance in the northeast corner was closed by a gate and stile. The hostelry that stood by the corner of Old Churchyard and Chapel Street was often known as The Stile House.

In the later seventeenth century, Church Stile House was the home of Captain Edward Tarleton, the progenitor of the family which was to play a very significant part in Liverpool's development over the
next century. By 1752 the house and its adjoining dwellings were part of the extensive estates of Mrs Sarah Clayton, a woman of great commercial acumen, who invested income from coal pits in property development in Liverpool – and who today is commemorated in the name of Clayton Square.

Paintings of the early eighteenth century show the House as a quaint black and white timbered building with a number of gables. By 1820 Church Stile House had been reduced to a fragment, in which its origins as a timber framed building are obvious, with the ends of the roof purlins visible in the gable wall and with a small jetty on the upper floor. The left-hand part of the structure has been added as a penthouse. There had been some re-glazing of the ground floor.

The sign board indicates that the inn was used as an office by the sexton and the clerk of the church. The sexton was responsible for the care of the churchyard, the fabric of the building and the digging of graves. The parish clerk kept the parish records, arranged dates for weddings and baptisms, and led the services and singing.

What Brierley does not show in the picture is the Gothic arch and gates that had been recently erected at the entrance to the churchyard. John Dennison was elected as Churchwarden in 1817 and, carried away by his importance, ignored all the normal constraints and 'entertained the notion that it was the function of the parishioners to pay and the churchwardens to spend and, up to this idea he fully acted'. [Picton, Memorials of Liverpool, vol. 2 p.339.] Money was spent on schools and buildings, including the erection of the arch into the church yard. Perhaps the townspeople were most galled by the weekly dinners given at the workhouse for Dennison's friends and Parish Officers. These dinners required sixteen dozen of port, £70 of Vidonia [a dry white wine produced in Tenerife], sixteen gallons of rum, together with brandy, jellies and lemons. He also claimed for 200 gallons of wine for the clergy which, with the other beverages, totalled £1,416 for the year. The Vestry refused to pass his accounts and he was prosecuted and fined at the Lancaster Assizes. Unsurprisingly, a move to compensate him for a sum of £2,000 met with little support.

Today, the arch and gate have gone, and the site of The Stile House is covered by the 1970s office block of St Nicholas' House. In 1891, the former burial ground was transformed into a memorial garden to Thomas Harrison, the shipping magnate.

View of the Parish Offices (late King's Arms Inn), and Talbot Hotel, Water Street, 1830

By the eighteenth century, Water Street (one of Liverpool's original seven streets, first known as Bonk Street and then Bank Street) had become one of the main thoroughfares of the town and a place where several important families had their homes. Amongst these was the splendid house of the Clayton family. The house was built c.1690–1700 by William Clayton, Mayor in 1689 and one

of the MPs for Liverpool from 1698 to 1708. With Sir Thomas Johnson, Clayton was instrumental in the passage of the Dock Bill. It was in this house that his fourth daughter, the redoubtable Sarah Clayton, was born in 1712. Sarah, who never married, went on to become a leading figure in the commercial and mercantile world of Liverpool, and attained great wealth which

she subsequently lost. Her portfolio of property developments included Clayton Square where she lived in the grandest house, a mansion located on the south side, which ended its days as the Jacey cinema showing 'adult films' and subsequently as the Shrine of the Blessed Sacrament.

The house in Water Street passed into the hands of Sarah's distant relative Thomas Tarleton, one of whose sons was General Sir Banastre Tarleton, a controversial but brilliant cavalry commander in the American War of Independence, and the subject of a striking portrait by Reynolds, a copy of which is in the Athenaeum. In 1786, the Tarleton family sold the house to Daniel Dale who opened it as the King's Arms Hotel in August of that year (see Gore's General Advertiser, 3 August 1786). Water Street also provided the location for a number of business houses and important hotels. The Talbot Hotel – originally the Golden Talbot – and the King's Arms filled the block between Fenwick Street and Lower Castle Street and were both establishments of some luxury. The Talbot, kept in 1825 by John Strout, was one of the principal coaching inns. The sign board on the left of the picture shows that it was a booking and tickets office for the mail coaches. The stables for the Talbot were in Fenwick Street but vehicular access was through the arch in Water Street. In the drawing these stables can be perceived through this arch.

In its day, in the second half of the eighteenth century, the King's Arms had been as equally important as its neighbour. It was kept by Daniel Dale, famous for his hospitality and bonhomie. An idea of the status held by the King's Arms is indicated by the fact that the emergency meeting of the Corporation following the destruction of the Exchange in 1795 was held there. One of the sights associated with the inn was the eccentric head waiter, Black Matthew, who always drank himself into insensibility on the King's birthday. After the death of Daniel Dale in 1804 Morris Jones assumed the proprietorship and, after his death, his widow continued the management of the hotel until it closed in 1822, with Matthew still in post.

At the time of the closure of the King's Arms the Vestry was concerned about the inadequate premises for its office and officers and the unnecessary expenditure caused by the dispersal of resources to various locations. As we have seen (see page 3) the Vestry or Parish, as it was known, had multiple and onerous responsibilities. These manifold duties required a large staff and it was realised that greater efficiency could be attained if the organisation were centralised. At the Vestry meeting of 3 May 1822, it was resolved 'to propose to the Common Council to build for the use of the Parish a suitable and convenient set of offices'.

Nothing further is recorded about this project, probably because an alternative had arisen. At the meeting held in October, it was announced that

The Churchwardens and Overseers, having agreed with the Corporation (the ground landlords) for the spacious and very convenient premises in Water Street (late the King's Arms) to which not only the respective boards connected with this Parish, but their officers, constables and servants will be speedily removed; and for the greater convenience of the Poor a large covered space will be appropriated to shelter them from the inclemencies of the weather, during their attendance on the Select Vestry and Overseers. [Liverpool Vestry Books, ed. H. Peet, 1915.]

This last suggestion was yet another example of the humane and benevolent attitude exhibited towards the Poor, by the Liverpool Vestry. Presumably, after the necessary work had been done on the former hotel, the move was carried out quickly – there is no further mention of it in the Vestry Books.

A view of St George's Church from the top of Pool Lane 1830

The fact that Brierley chose to present two views of this church is an indication of its novelty in the Liverpool landscape. Until 1699, when the Corporation acquired the lease of the former royal castle, the ground on which the church stood was within the curtilage of the fortress. About 1700, demolition of the castle began and part of the ground was earmarked by the Corporation as a site for new development. The rapidly expanding population of the town required additional ecclesiastical accommodation and it was resolved to build a new church on the cleared land. Finance for the new building was provided by the Corporation which, consequently, adopted St George's – the dedication was intended as a declaration of loyalty to the new Hanoverian regime – as the civic church. The original building was designed by Thomas Steers, whose elegant classical design showed remarkable competence in the English baroque style. Work began in 1726 and it was completed in 1734. The church, 80ft by 40ft, stood on a raised platform while the surrounding area was used as a market, especially for the sale of citrus fruits. There were two pavilions on the south-west and south-east corners of the platform. One of these had served as an office and stores for the market officials and the other seems to have been used as a town lock-up for the drunken and unruly. These were not replaced in the re-building of the church (see below).

A great deal of insight into the history of the church is given by the records of the Corporation. A committee of five members, including Steers, supervised the project. Clearly, they had decided opinions about the design. On 1 July 1724, estimates and several plans were presented and the Council resolved that they required 'a proper spire steeple at the west end and an alcove for a chancel on the east side or end', in the form of a small apse. By 5 November, when a model of the proposed church was presented, it was decided by the committee that '… the walls shall be plain, without pillars or pilasters and the windows after the same form as in Mr Shaw's model'. The completed building had lofty windows separated

A south west view of St George's Church, 1830

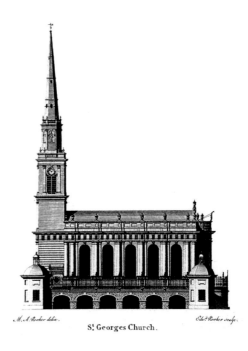

St Georges Church.

Illustration from Enfield's History of Liverpool 1773

by pilasters and the parapet was ornamented with urns. By 1729, arrangements for the supply of flagstones from a local delph were made and, three years later, plans were in hand for the market to the south of the church where a series of short-arched bays were provided. Shaw appears to have been both clerk of works and builder, though we learn later that an Edward Litherland did £60 worth of work on the steeple.

As the site of the castle was more extensive than was required for a church, the whole area was cleared and new buildings erected around the periphery. Several of the town's most important thoroughfares, Pool Lane, later South Castle Street, James Street, Castle Street and Lord Street converged on the piazza which was named Derby Square.

The consecration of the church took place on 1 August 1734. The Reverend Henry Wolstenholme was appointed chaplain with a salary of £50 a year and Mr Sewell, as curate, was to be paid £40. Income for the church was guaranteed by the letting of pews at an annual charge ranging from £43 8s. 0d. for the most favoured locations while a pew on the north side of the north gallery could be rented for £33 17s. 6d. Disputes over the ownership of pews, the right of inheritance and their arrangement bedevilled debates in the middle years of the century, provoking such remarkable decisions as 'The Town Clerk have one side of the Bailiff's wife's seat and the other be reserved for the Corporation' [4 Sept 1751].

Though the body of the church was built on the rock, the foundations of the steeple were in the filled castle ditch and unconsolidated foundations caused subsidence. Ralph Holland was instructed to take down the weathercock and carry out some repairs to the upper portion of the spire. By 1762, it was feared that the ruinous condition of the spire made it dangerous and it was surveyed but reported to be safe. A further survey was made in 1789 and though it was found to be more than three feet out of true, it was not considered to be liable to collapse. In 1791, remedial work was authorised. By 1809, the spire was so unsafe that it was taken down and between 1819 and 1825 the whole church was rebuilt to a new and simpler design, as shown in Brierley's pictures.

The new church, designed by John Foster the Younger, lacked the lofty grace of its predecessor. The side elevations were simple with a quasi frieze and a very solid parapet. The windows, increased from 5 to 6, were simple and the whole appeared lumpish and graceless. The new spire lacked the elegant symmetry of the Steer's design and was reminiscent of an elaborate wedding cake.

In Brierley's drawing of the church his elevated viewpoint is the top of Pool Lane facing in a westerly direction. To the right can be seen the newly rebuilt Castle Street where, in 1786, the western side was fronted with new and fashionable shops. It was originally intended that similar changes should be made on the other side. In the drawing the new shop fronts and the carefully designed upper storeys can be seen on the right of the picture. Some traces of these frontages are preserved, especially on the upper floors of the buildings at the south end of the street. In the south west view, the buildings on the left of the picture are those which lined the west side of Derby Square between James Street and Red Cross Street. The building on the left is the Fish Market (see page 139). Opposite the artist's viewpoint, Fenwick Street and Lower Castle Street can just be glimpsed beyond the spire of the church. Harrington Street appears on the right and the buildings in what was then called Castle Ditch, can be seen on the margin.

In 1897, St George's was no longer considered necessary as the residential population of the parish declined and the decision was made to demolish the church. It was decided that the Jubilee memorial to Queen Victoria should be erected on the site. The statues on the monument and the bronze panels on the plinth were the work of C. J. Allen and the domed baldacchino in Portland stone by F. M. Simpson and Willink & Thicknesse.

Old cottages, Silkhouse Lane, 1828

Old Cottages, Silkhouse Lane, Tythe Barn Street, 1830

Silkhouse Lane, which ran between Tithebarn Street and George Street to the east of Old Hall Street, is one of the thoroughfares of Liverpool which disappeared under the re-building programmes of the 1970s. However, its existence is commemorated in the name of the modern office block – Silkhouse Court.

Silk has always had an aura of mystery about it so it is perhaps understandable that so little is known about its manufacture in Liverpool. The importation of the fabric, manufactured in the

Orient and brought overland to Europe, dates from very early times. The early days of silk manufacture in England are obscure but by the end of the seventeenth century it was widespread, largely due to the arrival of Huguenot refugees who brought their skills to Spitalfields in London and later to other centres throughout England. The industry made great progress after the work of Sir Thomas Lombe, a wealthy woollen merchant of Norwich and London, who set up a mechanised mill in 1724 on the River Derwent at Derby. There are suggestions that some of this

establishment's hydraulic works and the water-driven machinery were the work of George Sorocold.

Evidence for the setting up of silk manufacture in Liverpool is sparse. A manuscript directory of 1734, in the collection of the Athenaeum, has no mention of the trade and no other reference has been found. A notice in Williamson's Advertiser for 18 June 1756 may indicate the establishment of the first silk house in the town.

To The Public

A Silk Manufactory is carried on in George Street, in this town by Mr THOMAS HOPKINS of LONDON; where such persons, either women or children (who are industriously inclined), may meet with such suitable encouragement, by applying to Mr WILLIAM HUGHES, Clerk of the said works

NB Such persons who are found begging (or otherwise unemployed) are desired to be directed as above.

Gore's Directory for 1766 lists Thomas Hopkins of Tithebarn Street as a silk thrower. In Enfield's An Essay towards a History of Liverpool [1773] he lists the importation of 15 bales of silk in the year 1770. It is unclear whether this figure refers

Old Cottages, Silkhouse Lane, Tythe Barn Street, 1830

*Silk throwing is the name given to the industrial process by which silk yarn is wound into skeins, then cleaned, twisted and placed on to bobbins. It is then made into thread by twisting two of more yarns together into thread.

to raw materials or finished cloth but may indicate the importation of materials for processing at Hopkin's Works. In either case, it suggests that silk was not of major concern in Liverpool. Hopkins are listed as silk 'throwsters' until 1774 at which point the name and, apparently, the trade disappears, though the silk house is included on Eyes' map dated 1796. On Horwood's survey of 1803, exemplary for its detail, no evidence of the silk manufactory is shown. Silk throwing* in the eighteenth century was largely organised on a domestic basis and it seems that Silkhouse Lane developed as a colony of silk workers. It seems reasonable to assume that the building shown here with the very unusual scrolled panel above the door is the original workshop with its adjacent cottages for the workers. Writing in 1875, J. A. Picton remarks that 'This avenue called Silkhouse Lane was formerly an antique-looking close surrounded by quaint old-fashioned buildings, one portion of which, afterwards converted into cottages, was the original 'Silk House.' [*op. cit.*]

Strand Street, 1830

Picture 1

Brierley's drawings of three views of Strand Street emphasise the varied nature of the Liverpool street scene in 1830. The buildings vary in style and date over the previous century and range from the utilitarian simplicity of the Eaves Biscuit Bakery [Brierley evidently mis-spells the name] to the comparative elegance of the public house next door, which has an early eighteenth century door case and an over-elaborate range of four Venetian windows – a feature of the late seventeenth century and the early decades of the Georgian period. Again, the artist was recording

a street which faced imminent and drastic change as the Improvement Act of 1825 brought about widespread widening of roads and demolition of old frontages. In the case of Strand Street, a whole new road linking it to Preeson's Row was proposed, though never built. Writing of this period, James Stonehouse, in his Streets of Liverpool says, 'In the improvements that took place in that neighbourhood all blocks of houses were swept away, and the present line of Strand Street was formed'. The maps show that, before the improvements, Strand Street continued the line

of the Goree Parade southward. Where there was an enlargement on the east side of George's Dock, three streets had been created: Sea Brow, Strand Street and Bird Street. After the intersection with Red Cross Street, only Strand Street continued to North Side, Old Dock. Crooked Lane intersected with Strand Street and it is the entrance to that alley which appears on the third picture.

A feature of Liverpool life in the early nineteenth century was the high degree of mobility shown by the population. There seems to have been an almost constant movement from premises to new addresses, while, at the same time, many businesses only continued to trade for relatively short periods. This is so marked a trend that it is useful to make a detailed consideration of Strand Street in the period between 1825 and 1829. A comparison of the occupants of property in the street between the 1825 Directory and that of 1829 shows a wholesale change with a remarkable degree of movement and impermanence. In 1825, Baines listed fifty premises in Strand Street with the names of their principal occupiers. By 1829, only four of these remained in the same location. In twenty-one cases the same name practising the same employment is to be found in new locations, often in nearby streets, perhaps because businesses were reluctant to lose contact with their old clientele. Several, for example, had moved to nearby Red Cross Street, which appears on the left-hand margin of the first picture. No fewer than twenty-four of the names listed in 1825 are not to be identified in the Gore's Directory for 1829 at any address in Liverpool. No doubt some of these had died but a large majority had disappeared without trace. It may have been the impending development of the Strand area that forced the shopkeepers and businesses to remove to new locations. It may have been the febrile and uncertain economic climate of the period which created a commercial world of uncertainty and impermanence and encouraged short term investment and quick turnover.

Brierley's drawings illustrate some of these changes and the arrival of some of the new occupiers. For example, the Globe Tavern does not appear in the earlier list but William Coyte is shown as a victualler in 1829 with an establishment in Bird Street, the lane adjoining the rear of Strand Street. J. Eaves & Co., ships' bread bakers are also a recent arrival, probably having taken over the business earlier owned by William McCarter at No. 17. The anchor smiths, C. H. Sharples at No. 30 - also had a yard in Byrom Street but do not appear in the 1825 Directory. Another new arrival was the rope-making and ships' chandlery of Thomas Gladston [sic] at No. 36. Something

of a mystery is presented by the building clearly labelled as that of H. Beckett and Co. This is not listed in 1825 and the directory of that year does not include an H. Becket, other than two ladies. There is an Oliver Beckett listed living in Stanley Street and working as a Broker. In 1829, Oliver Beckett and Co. are listed as agents at 32 Strand Street; on no occasion does the initial 'H' appear in the books and this may be another example of a mistake in Brierley's rendering of the scene.

Strand Street was an important component of the part of Liverpool, dedicated to serving the multifarious needs of sailors, ships and their cargoes. Nearby Bridge and Bromfield Streets were notorious for the presence of taverns and brothels. A rough analysis of the premises on Strand Street shows that sixteen were concerned with the sale of alcoholic liquors either on a wholesale or a retail basis. The needs of ships for ropes, equipment and repairs were met by ten dealers; six others were concerned with providing food in one form or another, and four supplied clothing both for seamen and landlubbers. Two businesses, a plumber and glazier and an earthenware merchant, supplied domestic needs, while a hairdresser provided for their tonsorial requirements. William Oulton, of No. 21, introduced a pleasantly rural note to the area. He was a Cow Keeper who would have had a small herd of cows in a shippon and would hawk the milk around the nearby streets. The trade of John Braithwaite is difficult to classify, as he is listed as merchant and tobacco pipe manufacturer.

Picture 2

Picture 3

China clay was mined in Cornwall and brought by sea to the Mersey where it was forwarded to Staffordshire by canal. A small portion was retained in the area and used for the making of pipes. This trade can be regarded as an off-shoot of the wider ceramic manufacture which was carried on in Liverpool, though this was in something of a decline at this period. Another unusual shop on Strand Street that is difficult to classify was that of Anne Patrick, the gunsmith, whose family business had been on the street but later moved to Pool Lane (See Pool Lane

page 131). Off the eastern side of Strand Street was the entry to Bold's Yard. Horwood's map of 1803 marks the sugar-boiling works of Mr Bold. By 1825 Nicholas Duckinfield Bold is described as a merchant with his counting house at No. 24 Strand Street. It is apparent that he had developed the area, possibly after the closure of his sugar works, for commercial purposes. It was occupied in 1825 by James McKune, a corn merchant, and John and Robert Thompson, who are described as general agents and agents to the Dumfries traders. By 1829 James McKune has disappeared from the

Directory and the Thompsons have removed to the east side of Salthouse Dock and had added Annan to their destinations in Lowland Scotland.

A view of old houses, Strand Street, corner of Red Cross Street, 1828

Strand Street was one of the main thoroughfares lining the Liverpool waterfront, running from the Goree Piazzas toward the Old Dock, North Side. It presented a wide variety of shops and businesses, especially those connected with maritime activities. Red Cross Street linked the Strand to Derby Square. Though the name of the street has a flavour of the Middle Ages about it, there is no evidence at all that there was any sort of cross in this area. In fact, Red Cross Street was a relatively late addition to the streets of Liverpool and originally called Tarleton New Street. Initially lined with substantial dwellings of mercantile families, by the middle of the eighteenth century it had a number of fashionable shops, though by 1830 these had declined in importance. The Crown Inn at its inland end was one of the principal coaching inns run by the Bretherton family. In 1825, amongst the many other businesses, were butchers and a cheesemonger who was also a dealer in Irish provisions. John Craig kept an eating house; Joseph Clingan was landlord of the St Patrick's Head public house, Joseph Robinson was a flax dresser, probably working with materials imported from Ireland. Keeping the maritime link, Simpson and Davies were well established ropemakers.

The clothing store, shown on the corner of Strand Street, was the shop run by Isabella Reed, the dressmaker, while the smaller shop next door was that of Isabella Rome, a clothes dealer. In the 1825 Directory, the Globe Tavern is instead listed by the name of the landlord Duncan McInnes; his postal address is given as 16 Strand Street. It can only be assumed that he did not choose to use the name Globe or that the name was only used in the interval between 1825 and 1828 when Brierley executed the picture.

It will be noted that once again the artist endeavoured to animate the scene by the inclusion of the couple walking, arm in arm, down Strand Street and by the depiction of the two horsed, two-wheeled wain, led by a carter in a traditional smock-frock and carrying his whip. As on other occasions, Brierley found it difficult to maintain proportions when it came to the representation of figures or animals. The stout gentleman in the large hat, who may be intended to represent Brierley himself, makes an appearance, although here he has abandoned his umbrella!

Old Cottages, Sweeting Street, commonly called Elbow Lane, 1830

If modern Liverpool has any 'quaint' corners the passageway of Sweeting Street would have to be included in them. The narrow street running from Dale Street through to Castle Street is little more than an alleyway and its route requires a sharp, right angled bend that suggested its alternative name of Elbow Lane – commonly used in Brierley's day. The street was the first in Liverpool to have its name painted on a sign and is named after Thomas Sweeting who was mayor in 1698.

Brierley's pictures seem to have a Dickensian air to them with houses, shops and businesses crowded together in the narrow passageways. This feeling is borne out by what we can discover about the community which lived and worked there and which seems to encompass many aspects of life in Liverpool at this time. Despite its short length, the street could boast three public houses, the Lancashire House, the Moseley Arms and the Sun. If this was not sufficient entertainment the man about town could drift into the billiard saloon kept by Thomas Botterill. If he then needed assistance to get home he could seek for a cab at the premises of William Millburn who kept a hackney carriage. If transport was not needed he might seek a gift for his beloved and a new pot of Bear's Grease Pomade for his own luxuriant locks at the Perfumers' shop kept by John Crossley. If he needed food he could seek it at the baker's shop run by Charles Currie. His shoes could be mended by William Hartley the shoemaker. If our 'Swell' needed legal advice he was spoilt for choice and could have applied to either John Clements or G. D. Bulmer, both attorneys, while Bulmer also practised as a Public Notary. He might seek employment with James Latham or Joseph Cheetham, both brokers, or with Joseph Robinson, a merchant, but also an agent for the Globe Insurance Company. At the end of another exhausting day he could seek a bed in the boarding house at No. 22, kept by Esther Rogers. All this was on offer within the confines of a street about two hundred yards in length, a statistic which brings home the cheek by jowl, hugger-mugger state of the town in Brierley's time.

Old Houses, Sweeting Street, commonly called Elbow Lane, 1830

It is worth noting that the building which lay within the crook of the elbow of Sweeting Street and fronted on to the junction of Castle Street and Dale Street was occupied by the bank of Clarke and Roscoe.

Like so many of the places that formed Brierley's subjects, in the next ten years Sweeting Street faced transformation. The whole area was altered by the rebuilding of the Dale Street façade of Queen Building and the introduction into the block, contained within the 'elbow', of the Royal Bank, whose Ionic façade still survives. A new thoroughfare, known as Queen Avenue, was built c.1837. In the 1840s, the early eighteenth century houses in Sweeting Street, shown in the drawings, were pulled down and replaced by sturdy blocks of offices and warehouses. Barned's Building (c.1840) in Sweeting Street dates from this rebuilding and survives as a good example of the commercial architecture of Liverpool in the early nineteenth century. It has enlarged windows to provide maximum daylight for the offices and wall cranes for handling goods in and out of the basement warehouse.

Today, even after the transformation, some of the little shops – especially the tailors – still survive and the whole area retains something of an antiquated air.

Four street scenes

Old House Mersey Street corner of Salt House Lane, 1830.

However, the reference to Salt House Lane gives the opportunity to describe a very important aspect of the development of Liverpool in the eighteenth and early nineteenth centuries. Indeed, John Holt, writing in the late eighteenth century, remarks 'The salt trade is generally acknowledged to have been the Nursing Mother and to have contributed more to the first rise, gradual increase and the present flourishing state of the Town of Liverpool, than any other Article of Commerce'. Some modern historians are agreed that the profits of the 'Triangular Trade' in coal and salt within the Mersey estuary far surpassed the profits which accrued to Liverpool from the infamous triangle of trade between the port, West Africa and the West Indies.

Salt has always been an important ingredient in human diet and, in addition, was an essential commodity for the preservation of food and for culinary and industrial purposes. The main supply was from coastal salt pans in the Mediterranean region, southern France and the Biscay coast. English salt was extracted from various brine wells or wiches to be found in Cheshire and the West Midlands but these made a comparatively minor contribution to the provision of salt in England. The discovery of rock salt in 1670 at Marbury in Cheshire revolutionised production. Rock salt was dissolved, preferably in sea water, and evaporated over coal fires. The salt produced

In his Memorials of Liverpool, the historian J. A. Picton writes [1875] of Thomas Street, 'The four streets running from Pool Lane to Paradise Street have nothing very remarkable in their history. Thomas Street and Atherton Street until very recently preserved many specimens of their original architecture which are now fast passing away.' It was probably the desire to record these four views, simply to save for posterity the style of the older parts of Liverpool, which made James Brierley select these subjects. Apart from their intrinsic interest in displaying the architecture of Liverpool's streets, they do not show any buildings which can be identified as having a particular merit.

Old Houses Thomas Street, corner of Love Lane, 1828

was of good quality and could be refined much more cheaply than that obtained from the wiches. [THLC Lancashire Coal, Cheshire Salt and the rise of Liverpool, T. C. Barker, vol. 103, 1951]

This gave a new significance to the availability of stocks of coal. The proximity to navigable waterways on which the two bulky and heavy commodities of rock salt and coal could be carried ensured that refineries were established at Frodsham Bridge and later at Dungeon Point, Hale, on the north bank of the Mersey estuary and at Liverpool. Salt had been made in Liverpool for many years. There is a reference in an Inquisition of 1348 to a 'Saltousmorre' [Saltens' Moor]. The commercial processing of the mineral can be identified in 1600 while, in 1611, the Town books contain a reference to a motion to encourage the settlement of 'one Atkinson' who could make white salt at 12d. per bushel.

The Blackburne family came to dominate salt production in Liverpool from the 1690s. They were connected to the owners of Hale Hall and were important salt shippers in Northwich. By 1696, two brothers, Jonathan and John, were petitioning the Corporation to establish 'a shed, keeling house and quay near the intended salt works on the south shore at Liverpool.' In the next year, we have the first reference to the Dungeon salt works, which they also operated.

It was the Blackburnes' works which gave its name to Salthouse Dock. The works filled much of the quay on the east side of the dock, and comprised two blocks of buildings, each of two structures, separated by the range of salt pans. The works were closed in 1796 and removed to Garston Creek in response to complaints from the town of the noxious nature of the fumes and smoke emitted. On Merseyside production of salt for export increased from 150,000 tons in 1800 to 1,000,000 tons in 1870. A further 116, 000 tons were produced for domestic consumption.

Salt was a vital raw material for the new chemical industry, especially for the manufacture of sulphuric acid [copperas]. This manufacture was introduced at the factory on Copperas Hill owned by the Hughes family in c.1750. Later, the new Leblanc process was introduced at the works of James Muspratt at Vauxhall in 1820. This was one of the foundations of the chemical industry in the area, though later production was transferred to the upper Mersey estuary at Runcorn and Widnes.

John Blackburne and another salt man, John Ashton, were the main protagonists for the building of the Sankey Brook or St Helen's Canal, often described as Britain's first canal, which was designed to bring coal from the St Helens area to the navigable waters of the Mersey.

In Liverpool, the Blackburne family occupied a large mansion of two wings and a central block that they had built in Hanover Street and they became deeply involved in municipal affairs, John Blackburne becoming Mayor of Liverpool in 1760. His son, of the same name, built a new mansion in Hope Street and subsequently moved to Orford Hall near Warrington.

Old Houses, Frederick Street, near St Thomas's Church, 1830.

A view of old houses, Trafford Lane, 1828

A View of Old Houses, Trafford Lane, 1828.

Trafford Lane, or, as it was sometimes known, Trafford Weint, was a small street that continued the line of John Street, Marshall Street and Love Lane to the eastern end of the Old Dock. The name of the street commemorated Henry Trafford, a distinguished contributor to the affairs of Liverpool who, in 1738, loaned money to the Corporation to enable it to meet the costs of building a new pier.

Although Brierley entitles this picture Trafford Lane, the road received a new name in 1829 when it became part of the new South John Street after the Corporation obtained Parliamentary consent to widen and extend Marshall Street, Love Lane and Trafford Lane. This was the most ambitious scheme of street improvement yet attempted in Liverpool which, when implemented, cost a total of £20,383. Two very different styles of building are apparent in the picture. The main

block appears to be of late seventeenth or early eighteenth century date, predating the opening of the street in 1740. The more imposing house beyond the terrace with its front door raised above the street and with the door contained in an elaborate door case is of a mid-eighteenth century date. The house displays the Georgian love of symmetry and balance in design and was the sort of house being built to reflect the increasing prosperity of the town and of its merchants. One of the redundant cannon barrels used to protect the buildings from passing wagons can be seen.

Baines' Directory of 1825 lists the occupants of the houses in Trafford Lane. No. 1 was occupied by Gardner and Harding, wine and spirit merchants. They combined their trade in alcoholic beverages with being agents for the Harford and Bristol Brass Company. Next door to them was the yard and workshop of James McClumpha, a joiner. John Wilson, a cotton bag and sacking warehouseman, was at No. 8, while at No. 9 was the establishment of Hugh Locklin who, in another bizarre combination, was both a hairdresser and a sack-cloth seller. The host of the Montrose Tavern, at No. 10, was Alexander Harris who, by 1829, had added work as a shipwright to his status as licensee. At No. 11 was a store for Henry and Thomas Wilson, the linen-drapers, whose main premises were on the North Side of Old Dock. By 1829 they had relocated their shop to Duke Street. Samuel Langshaw, a dealer in ale, wine, spirits, beer and porter was at No. 12. Adjoining his premises was the home and offices of a West India merchant, Andrew Clark, Junior, who, by 1829, had moved to Woodside. The last house in the lane was the office of S. Ravenscroft and Company, master porters.

Brierley creates a small mystery in the square sign board on the first building in Trafford Lane. Though difficult to read in Brierley's version, it appears to give the name S. Wood and the occupation of surgeon. The building next door has the barber's pole sign, a reminder of the close connection between the two occupations. However, no record of a surgeon named Wood can be found in any of the appropriate directories, nor do these list a surgeon named Wood or any other surgeon in Trafford Lane at any other time. It is possible that the sign is a flight of fancy on the part of the artist, but most of the other shops and businesses for which he shows a sign or name board can be identified so that it seems unlikely that this establishment did not exist.

Brierley's drawing was an obituary for the old Trafford Lane, one of the many Liverpool streets which, at this time, faced redevelopment and change. This particular view is difficult to orientate, and it is only because of the glimpse of the tower of St Thomas' Church that we can determine the direction in which the artist was looking. Though it is not very clear, he was located at the corner of King Street, looking south across the east end of the Old Dock and down Frederick Street to the church. It seems strange that nothing of the dock appears in the picture but study of the maps of the period shows that this might have been possible.

Further Reading

Various articles in this bibliography are marked THLC, that is, the Transactions of the Historic Society of Lancashire and Cheshire. Since its foundation at Liverpool in 1848, this, the most distinguished of the local historical societies, has published an annual volume of Transactions. These publications contain a wealth of material on the city and only a few selected articles have been listed here. Reference to the index volume, published in 2000 will show the variety of studies available.

Ainsworth & Jones, In the Footsteps of Peter Ellis, Liverpool Historical Society 2013Ascott, Lewis & Power, Liverpool 1600–1750, Liverpool 2006.

Barker T. C., Lancashire Coal, Cheshire Salt and the Rise of Liverpool, THLC Vol 103 1951.

Belchem J. ed., Liverpool 800, Liverpool 2008.

Bickerton T., Medical History of Liverpool, Liverpool 1937.

Blease L., Poor Law in Liverpool, THLC vol. 61 1909.

Brooke R., Liverpool as it Was, Liverpool 2003.

Brown & de Figueriedo, Religion & Place, London 2008.

Chandler G., Liverpool, London 1957.

Enfield W., History of Liverpool, Warrington 1773.

Giles C., Building a Better Society, London 2008.

Giles & Hawkins, Storehouses of Empire, London 2004.

Good J. M., Dissertation on Employment in Workhouse London, 1798.

Lewis D., The Churches of Liverpool, Liverpool 2001.

Moss ed. Brazendale, Georgian Liverpool, Lancaster 2007.

Muir R. A., History of Liverpool, Liverpool 1907.

Nicholson S. ed., The Changing Face of Liverpool, Liverpool 2007.

Peet H., Liverpool Vestry Books, Liverpool 1915.

Peet H., Thomas Steers, THLC vol. 82, 1930.

Picton J. A., Liverpool Municipal Records, Liverpool 1883/6.

Picton J. A., Memorials of Liverpool, London 1875.

Power M., Creating a Port, THLC vol. 149 2000.

Touzeau, J., Rise & Progress of Liverpool, Liverpool 1910.

Ritchie-Noakes N., Liverpool's Historic Waterfront, RCHM 1984.

Sharples J., Liverpool Pevsner's Architectural Guide, Yale 2004.

Sharples & Stonard, Built on Commerce, London 2008.

Sheperd J., History of Liverpool Medical Institute, Liverpool 1979.

Stewart-Brown S., Liverpool in the Reign of Charles II, Liverpool.

Stonehouse J., The Streets of Liverpool Liverpool, Liverpool, 2002.

Tibbles A., Catalogue of Maritime Paintings, Liverpool 1999.

Troughton & Corrie, History of Liverpool, Liverpool 1816.

Wilson A., Cultural Identity of Liverpool, THLC vol. 147, 1998.

Wilson A., William Roscoe, Liverpool 2008.